GUIDE TO THE
MANAGEMENT
GURUS

GUIDE TO THE MANAGEMENT GURUS

SHORTCUTS TO THE IDEAS OF LEADING MANAGEMENT THINKERS

CAROL KENNEDY

CENTURY
BUSINESS

First published in 1998 by Century Ltd
Random House, 20 Vauxhall Bridge Road, London SW1V 2SA

Random Century Australia (Pty) Limited
20 Alfred Street, Milsons Point, Sydney
New South Wales 2061, Australia

Random Century New Zealand Limited
18 Poland Road, Glenfield
Auckland 10, New Zealand

Random Century South Africa (Pty) Limited
Endulini, 5a Jubilee Road, Parktown 2193, South Africa

Random House UK Limited Reg. No. 954009

Papers used by Random House UK Limited are natural, recyclable products made from wood grown in sustainable forests. The manufacturing processes conform to the environmental regulations of the country of origin.

ISBN 0 7126 7950 2

CONTENTS

INTRODUCTION

The Age of the Guru

There is a limit to the number of original ideas in any field of human activity, and management is no exception. After all, it is said that there are no more than half a dozen basic plots throughout the whole world of fiction and drama. Some of the most enduring themes of management were conceived centuries before commercial or industrial management was born – let alone the concept of the management guru with his or her prescriptives for performance.

Machiavelli's *The Prince*, written at the height of Renaissance Florence, is still a classic text on leadership and the uses of power (and inspired a popular management book of the 1960s by Antony Jay). The translator of its bestselling Penguin edition, George Bull, says *The Prince*'s precepts are 'perfectly applicable to the actions of captains of industry or budding entrepreneurs,' citing as just one example Machiavelli's advice that when a ruler seizes a state (or a new chief executive moves into a company), he must do the hardest things first. 'The new ruler must determine all the injuries that he will need to inflict. He must inflict them once and for all, and not have to renew them every day. In that way he will be able to set men's minds at rest, and win them over to him when he confers benefits.' Every takeover king has instinctively practised that.

Further back in history, the basic human responses to work and responsibility were articulated by Plato and

Aristotle in their differing views of man; the one believing
authoritarian direction was needed if anything of value was
to be accomplished, the other that man as a 'social' or
'political' animal required a sense of participation in his own
destiny. In the 1960s Douglas McGregor dressed up the
concepts with sociological research into industrial practice
and presented them as Theory X and Theory Y – authoritarian versus democratic management. It became one of the
great management theories of all time.

Digging even deeper into antiquity, management writers
have adapted the wisdom of Taoism to the modern executive office. There is even a book on management in
Shakespeare and jokey exercises on Genghis Khan and Attila
the Hun as business tacticians. No doubt the Roman
emperors will one day yield a book on leadership strategy.

Variations on ideas, of course, are infinite – or can be
made to seem so. It is this which accounts for the vast num-
bers of management books that pour annually from publishing houses on both sides of the Atlantic, and for the
lucrative lecture circuits and all the paraphernalia of com-
mercially packaged wisdom that bring handsome incomes –
indeed, millionaire status – to the leading management
guru. The explosion of management advice has been phenomenal – from 771 business books published in the UK in
1975 to nearly 3,000 in 1996, a market worth £35m, and in
the US close to $1bn.

The management guru whose precepts are bought as the
key to success is essentially a phenomenon of the last 40 to
50 years. Before World War II, when, as Peter Drucker has
recalled, 'all the books on management filled no more than
a modest shelf' – perhaps 70 in all languages except Japanese
– the thinkers on management who won the admiration of
their peers could be numbered on the fingers of one hand.

Several were career businessmen whose management wisdom was distilled into books long after they had learned it
on the job; notably Alfred P. Sloan of General Motors, who
built the world's largest corporation out of a medium-sized,
ailing automobile manufacturer, and Chester Barnard of
AT&T, who wrote what remained for many years the
definitive text on the functions of the executive. Sloan's

memoir, *My Life With General Motors*, is still revered, 35 years after publication and more than 70 years after the events it chronicled, as the classic exposition of how to create a great business enterprise by applying the principles of total marketing and decentralization.

In Britain, the lone management theorist in the 1930s was Lyndall Urwick, who had been converted to 'scientific management' as an officer in the Flanders trenches by reading the works of Frederick W. Taylor, the progenitor of time and motion study. In 1934 Urwick set up Britain's first management consultancy, Urwick Orr and Partners.

Others who worked away in the interwar years, reacting against Taylor's mechanistic approach by studying the human element in organizations and the springs of motivation, including Elton Mayo with his experiments at Western Electric's Hawthorne plant in Chicago (a forcing house for later gurus), did not publish their findings until the 1950s or 1960s. Then, backed by distinguished academic appointments in North American universities, they became almost instant gurus.

Management gurus are overwhelmingly a US phenomenon, bred out of the great business schools such as Harvard, Stanford and the Sloan School of Management at Massachusetts Institute of Technology (MIT). The UK can boast only one guru of world class, the philosophical Charles Handy, who is withdrawing from the study of business organizations to focus on wider questions of capitalism and society, though the ideas of earlier, underrated thinkers such as Reg Revans – the originator of action learning – continue to resonate.

As with inventions, Britain has given birth to several key management theories and seen them developed elsewhere. The principle of separating value-adding from non-value-adding activities, which lies behind re-engineering, the value chain and much else, was first developed by an obscure ICI work study researcher, while several of today's dominant management themes, including group working and the impact of technology on employees, were pioneered by the Tavistock Institute in London's Bloomsbury district.

Hugely but quietly influential over the 50 years of its existence, the Tavistock, a hybrid research establishment which was set up to help postwar organizational reconstruction, has never possessed the flair of the US business schools in marketing ideas. 'Socio-technical systems,' in Tavistock-speak, does not have the ring of 're-engineering,' though it took a more humanistic approach to technology-driven processes; something Hammer and his disciples have adopted only belatedly. Professor Enid Mumford, a Tavistock council member, has described re-engineering as 'the poor man's version of socio-technical systems – restructuring without any human element.' Elements of Tavistock research also paved the way for teamworking and empowerment and contributed to Japanese quality circles and to the admired group work practices at Saab and Volvo.

In mainland Europe, the concept of the management guru is almost unknown except for a cluster of high-powered thinkers at INSEAD, the international business school at Fontainebleau, near Paris. Here, some significant theories are being developed in the field of strategic management by a Korean-born academic, W. Chan Kim, and a fellow professor of strategy, Renée Mauborgne. Their concepts of innovation thinking and of 'fair process' – capturing the loyalty and creativity of employees through transparent management decision-making – provoked international interest after their publication in *Harvard Business Review*.

INSEAD also has its own leadership guru-in-waiting, Dutch-born Manfred Kets de Vries, who takes a psychologist's approach to the subject and has published a popular book on leadership and stress, *Life and Death in the Executive Fast Lane*. Yves Doz is another INSEAD heavyweight thinker, who has linked up as an author with the ubiquitous Gary Hamel of California. The Anglo-American dominance of management theory is such, however, that the INSEAD professors are likely to remain respected academics rather than international gurus.

Hamel, a new addition to this book, is a former Stanford professor who had been lecturing unobtrusively on strategy at London Business School for a decade before shooting to virtually overnight guru status after publication of *Competing for the Future* in 1994. This identified the concept of core competencies and strategic intent which have become his trademark subjects. Now he ranks almost in the Peters-Porter league as a highly paid management speaker, in demand all over the world and on video-conference linkups. Meanwhile, his co-author, Indian-born C.K. Prahalad, while also active on the conference circuit and a respected theorist, does not command anything like the same attention from the market.

The guru phenomenon is also curiously absent from Japan and the other erstwhile 'tiger' economies of the Pacific Rim. These appear, until recently, to have generated world-beating success in business without benefit of home-grown gurus, unless one counts the heads of Honda, Sony and Matsushita, who have achieved a certain guru status through the way they run their companies. (Japan's one great obeisance to management gurus remains its homage to America's W. Edwards Deming and Joseph Juran, who converted the Japanese in the 1950s to the principles of quality control.) Since the word 'guru' (a Sanskrit derivation meaning weighty and extended to mean a Hindu priest), originated in the East, one may ask why Eastern businesses have been able to manage pretty well without them. The inescapable conclusion is that in the West everything has to be marketed before it is taken seriously – and that goes for the whole management improvement business. Not surprisingly, a number of leading US academics who enjoy high guru status dislike being tagged with the word, though nearly all have highly commercial consultancies and are no strangers to marketing their own skills.

How are gurus born or created? Many a management writer and professor of business studies has laboured towards the elusive goal without ever coming close to it, while others seem to be elevated to guru status without even trying. You can be a highly successful author, invent a genre of books like Kenneth Blanchard's *The One-Minute Manager*, and still not approach gurudom, however much in demand you are on the lecture or after-dinner circuit.

You can be a captain of industry with a brilliant track record at turning companies around and a gift for the best-selling memoir, like Sir John Harvey-Jones, Lee Iacocca or the late Harold Geneen, and spend a lucrative retirement passing on high-priced pearls of wisdom to business or TV audiences – yet still not rank as a true guru.

You can make a career out of futurology like Alvin Toffler and John Naisbitt in the US, or Francis Kinsman in the UK, and be quoted for years on phrases like 'Future Shock', 'The Third Wave' or 'Megatrends' – yet ultimately fail the guru test. (Gurus have to be measured against the hard problems of here and now: Charles Handy's explorations of the future are solidly rooted in present dilemmas, and besides, he won his spurs as an expert on business organizations.)

You can beaver away for years in university or business school back offices, producing brilliant theses and papers that might eventually become the only work of their kind on, say, long-range planning in the electronics industry, or the development of an Asian management style. In the past that might have brought guru status in time, starting with a small circle of fellow-academics and filtering into the business world; today's harsh demands of media and marketing combine to make it very difficult for the quiet thinker or teacher to achieve gurudom.

The three leading gurus in the world today are generally acknowledged to be Peter Drucker, Tom Peters and Michael Porter. The first is in his late eighties and, by virtue of his long reputation and productivity over the years, immune to the pressures of the video age, though he pursues an active international round of seminars. The others are in their fifties and – though Porter is a Harvard academic – they have grown up with telecommunications, marketing hype and the need to add a gloss of show-business to selling their wares.

Watch Tom Peters (he and Porter vie with each other for the highest lecture fees in the business) pacing the platform, pouring megawatts of energy into his exposition, his shirt dark with sweat after only a few minutes. He is more an evangelist of business ideas than a teacher; he entertains and inspires as well as informs. Porter is somewhat lower key in style but engages his audience with humour and painlessly lures them into dense intellectual concepts with brilliantly packaged analytic models and flip-charts.

Packaging, indeed, is half the art, or even more, of becoming a modern guru. As *Business Week* reported in the summer of 1990, some academics and consultants in the US regard Porter's concepts on competitive strategy as gimmicky, but nearly all acknowledge that he is 'a master at packaging and marketing ideas.' Porter himself talks about the importance of 'the Michael Porter brand', and this is emphatically the trend today, to become as identified with a business theory as Porter is with competitive strategy and competitive advantage. The underlying truths may be as old as trading itself, but Porter has branded them, and as such they are supremely saleable. By mid-1990, *Business Week* reported, his royalties on four books, beginning with *Competitive Strategy* in 1980, had brought him over $2m.

Gurudom can start with one stunningly successful book, a book that every executive must be seen with. The prime example here is, of course, Peters' and Waterman's *In Search of Excellence* – still reprinting in its original format 16 years after first publication, despite the fact that two-thirds of its 'excellent' companies have since faded from glory and that Peters himself opened his second book, *Thriving on Chaos*, with the cheeky statement: 'There are no excellent companies.'

Of the two authors, however, only Peters has chosen to haul himself up to the top rung of international gurus; his temperamentally opposite co-author Bob Waterman, a quiet, reflective Californian, prefers a less stressful, time-pressured existence. Waterman's first solo book, *The Renewal Factor*, is regarded by some management teachers as a far deeper, more intellectually rigorous work than Peters' best-selling *Thriving on Chaos*, but it is Peters who commands the global 'branding' factor and the huge fees that go with it.

Of course branding, packaging and a flair for show-business are only part of the answer. What marks out the real guru – the one who will be read in business schools and boardrooms – from the business hero turned media celebrity, or the author who hits on a jokey formula like the

One-Minute Manager or the business strategy of Genghis Khan, is the ability to generate original, durable thinking on the hard matter of managing people and resources.

All the gurus whose ideas are summarized in this book (and no summaries can do full justice to a lifetime of thinking: their key books should be read) meet this requirement, even out-of-date theorists like F. W. Taylor and Max Weber. Their ideas were not only important in their time; they have been adapted and built on for generations, even if they have been partly destroyed in order to use the bricks again. And in some quarters they have not been wholly destroyed: Robert Waterman muses that many more managers are Taylorists at heart than would ever admit it.

Gurus broadly divide into those with one Big Idea – Edward de Bono's lateral thinking is a perfect example, out of which he has spun a sparkling web of books, international seminars and blue-chip consultancy – and those, like Peter Drucker and Charles Handy, whose fizzing intellects spray ideas in all directions; about the future of work and society, new designs for organizations, geopolitical shifts and managing change. Michael Porter's emphasis on competitive strategy puts him basically in the first category (a Big Idea can have endless spin-offs), while Tom Peters shows signs of developing into a multi-ideas guru.

All have one thing in common: they build on each other's ideas and on their own. There is nothing remotely discreditable or plagiaristic in this: it is only what historians and philosophers have done down the ages. The Californian professor of management William Ouchi had a tremendous success with his 1981 book *Theory Z*, which used the terminology of McGregor's Theory X and Theory Y, going a step beyond Theory Y to describe, with case studies, the kind of consensus-seeking management which has succeeded so brilliantly in Japan. McGregor himself had begun to formulate a Theory Z, but did not have time to develop it in depth before he died. Richard Pascale, in *Managing on the Edge*, says McGregor's last theory was quickly forgotten, and it was reborn independently as the archetype of Japanese business practice.

Another typical piece of guru language – gurus can be

identified by their ability to invent terms that go into the management vocabulary, like Theory X, re-engineering, the psychological contract or lateral thinking – that has gone through many retreads is 'adhocracy.' The term, meaning, roughly, the opposite of bureaucracy, a flexible sort of task force that crosses the frontiers within organizations, first surfaced in Warren Bennis' *The Temporary Society* in 1968, gained wider currency in Alvin Toffler's *Future Shock* in 1970, emerged independently in Henry Mintzberg's *The Structuring of Organizations* in 1979 and, most recently, formed the subject of an entire short book by Robert Waterman. Charles Handy has also explored the implications of the term. 'We all build on each other's work,' smiled Waterman when asked about the genesis of his title.

Everybody, for two generations of gurudom, has drawn somewhere on Drucker, that monumental quarry of management wisdom and original thought. Even Theories X and Y, as McGregor acknowledged, synthesized the ideas of others, including some which Drucker had presented in three early books – *Concept of the Corporation, The New Society*, and *The Practice of Management*. Peters and Waterman, too, said that much of what they discovered in identifying their principles of excellence had first been aired by Drucker 30 years before.

There are few great themes of management, just as there are few great plots in fiction. Probably the richest vein, and the one that has attracted most theorists over the years, involves the human side of management, understanding what motivates men and women to work and to strive for better performance. Frederick Taylor thought that efficiency was all, and that it could be measured and mastered by a stopwatch; later gurus tackled more complex, deeper themes.

The first area to be explored in management writing, by the French mining manager Henri Fayol at the turn of the century, was the function of management itself; still a fertile field as the late 20th century continues to be obsessed with how to manage change and discontinuity. Another early and long-lived theme is organizational theory, including hierarchies and the need or otherwise for them, and the now fashionable 'flatter management structures' which are supposed to 'empower' the employee farther down the line. 'Empowerment' is a new subdivision of this genre (or maybe a new word for an old concept) and the formidable Rosabeth Moss Kanter, who formerly edited the *Harvard Business Review* along with teaching, consultancy and writing influential books, has explored all that this implies for releasing the forces of change and innovation within organizations.

In the late 1990s, the growing emphasis on 'intellectual capital' – the sum of employee talent and accumulated knowledge in a company – created a new theory of 'knowledge management.' No single guru has yet been identified with the field, though the business school at the University of California in Berkeley has created the first chair of knowledge management, held in 1997 by the Japanese professor Ikujiro Nonaka. The subject, a natural for the information age and 'knowledge workers' (a term first coined by Peter Drucker in 1969), was business-led, most notably by Skandia, the Swedish financial services company, and its potential as management theory was initially spotted by a *Fortune* magazine writer, Thomas A. Stewart, in the first of several 1997 books with the same title, *Intellectual Capital*. It has since been the subject of a spate of conferences, seminars and heavy management reports, and a number of US companies have followed Skandia in appointing Chief Knowledge Officers or similar titles.

The search for better organizational performance is an almost inexhaustible field, with spin-offs ranging from strategy to marketing to company culture to the art of the mission statement. In Britain, the Strategic Management Centre set up by Ashridge Management College is breeding a stable of potential gurus in strategy and corporate missions, headed by Andrew Campbell and Michael Goold. If anything could hinder their progress to guru status it is probably their prolific output of books, and the changing permutations of authors. Gurus rarely come in pairs and even more rarely stay in pairs: Anthony Athos, who co-authored *The Art of Japanese Management* with Richard Pascale in 1981, has vanished from view, and Pascale took nine years before bursting into print again – most successfully – with *Managing on the Edge*. He is now firmly established as a solo guru of fast-growing influence.

Leadership is a field that has attracted surprisingly few gurus, perhaps because its mystique, like that of monarchy, is hard to expose to daylight; leadership, ultimately, may be in the eye of the beholder. The US leadership guru James McGregor Burns, a political scientist and active campaigner for President John F. Kennedy, described leadership as 'one of the most observed and least understood phenomena on earth.' Burns was the first to identify the distinction between 'transactional' and 'transformational' leadership, explaining that the first is a tacit agreement to exchange one benefit for another (i.e., jobs for votes) while a leader of the second type engages in a deeper relationship with his followers. 'The transforming leader looks for potential motives in followers, seeks to satisfy higher needs. . . .'

Why Burns has not become as famous in the field as Warren Bennis, who started out as an organizational theorist, is curious, but only one of many anomalies in what may be called the greater and lesser guru syndrome. Some do progress from lesser to greater status: one example in this new edition is John P. Kotter, professor of organizational behaviour and human resource management at Harvard Business School. When this book was first published in 1991 he had a couple of respected books to his name on managerial and leadership qualities, but in the intervening years, he has become one of the world's top authorities on leadership in organizations, and a highly sought-after speaker on the international circuit.

Sometimes excellent work just fails to turn its progenitors into gurus, however, especially when there are established stars in the field. The pairing of Harvard professor Christopher Bartlett and INSEAD professor Sumantra Ghoshal produced, in 1989, a book called *Managing Across Borders*, that was of much more practical value to managers in multinationals than Kenichi Ohmae's later, more abstract work, *The Borderless World*. Yet Ohmae still has guru status, and his book, though undermined in its thesis that nationalism is on the wane by the savage war in former Yugoslavia, rides on a reputation created by his earlier works, *The Mind of the Strategist* and *Triad Power*.

Bartlett and Ghoshal delved into case studies as fascinating in their application to global-marketing companies as those on Japanese and US companies in *The Art of Japanese Management*. As the single market in Europe becomes a reality and a challenge, they too may find their hour as did Pascale and Athos when US industrialists were running scared of the Japanese threat and desperate to learn how to defeat it. Timing is of the essence in achieving gurudom.

Timing; originality; forcefulness; a gift for self-promotion and perhaps above all else, the ability to encapsulate memorably what others immediately recognize as true – these are the marks of the modern management guru. Peters and Waterman created the first mass-selling management book – the one everyone needed to read – by packaging some fundamental truths in snappy slogans like 'stick to the knitting.' Beneath the glossy paintwork, however, was a solidly built motor that, while not entirely original in every part, would probably last as long as the heavy-duty classics of Chandler, Barnard and Mayo – indeed, was partly cannibalized from those very vehicles.

One thing is certain: in an age of incessant searching for a grail of business and personal success that recedes as surely as Gatsby's green light into the distance, of the making of management gurus there is no foreseeable end.

Since this book was first published in 1991, the guru industry has burgeoned in all directions and interest in the phenomenon, if tinged with healthy scepticism, has magnified. Seven additional gurus are included in this edition: Meredith Belbin of the eponymous team-building technique; Gary Hamel; Michael Hammer of re-engineering fame; marketing guru Philip Kotler; John Kotter; Robert Kaplan and David Norton, the partnership behind the Balanced Business Scorecard, and Peter Senge, progenitor of the 'learning organization.'

Gurus have also proliferated in vaguely business-related areas of personal development, the best-known of these being Stephen Covey, the Mormon who has built a multimillion-dollar industry out of his 'Seven Habits of Highly Effective People.' President Bill Clinton and members of his administration have bought into the Covey prescriptives, which are based on character-building exercises not so far removed from those associated with the ur-guru of Victorian self-help, Samuel Smiles.

As the guru and mini-guru industry has boomed, management fads and fashions flare across the horizon so fast and frequently that it becomes increasingly difficult to tell which will burn out quickly and which, if any, will last. Hugh Macdonald, a former academic at MIT and Cranfield School of Management, once calculated the lifespan of a management fad at 11–12 years from its first germination in academic papers through the *imprimatur* of the *Harvard Business Review*, then the best-selling book, the subject-matter of lectures and conferences and the basis of a lucrative consultancy. (Oddly, the average lifespan of companies has been put at a similar age, around 13 years.) Fads have such a velocity today, however, that Adrian Wooldridge and John Micklethwait, authors of *The Witch Doctors* (1995), a witty dissection of the management theory industry, put the survival of some at no more than a year.

Inevitably, the curve of interest dips and the theory then has to be replaced by an advanced or different model. Some theories just fade slightly, leaving ghosts of themselves, like Peters' and Waterman's eight rules of excellence, in which 'stick to the knitting' was reborn a decade later as core competencies, having never really been abandoned; others, like re-engineering, may be tested to destruction in the real world of management and have to be relaunched.

By Macdonald's system, re-engineering has already run its course: born at MIT and the neighbouring consultancy CSC Index in the early 1980s; *HBR* article in 1990; bestseller in 1993; disillusionment setting in around 1995 with a 70 per cent failure rate and a fatal association in people's minds with cost-cutting and downsizing. But the principle does work well in certain types of organization, and its godfather Mike Hammer has had a Damascene conversion to understanding that it is people, not processes alone, that make change work.

Ultimately, time and experience sort the wheat from the chaff. The theories that have best stood this test are those of the behavioural scientists such as Elton Mayo, Abraham Maslow, Douglas McGregor and Frederick Herzberg, whose work lit the way to a deeper understanding of what makes people function best in office, shop or factory. Their ideas gave rise to empowerment, self-managed teams, and the sort of relationship between employer and employee that could survive in a very different world of work from that of the 1950s or the 1960s.

Colin Ions, human resources director of the UK brewing giant Courage, draws 'immense support' from the big ideas of Maslow and McGregor – the latter, he claims, is 'all about trust,' a key buzzword of the late 1990s, while Maslow's 'hierarchy of needs' still underpins employee motivation.

Their books may be out of print but their theories shifted the management landscape and are rooted in timeless truths about human nature. Will the same be said a generation hence about re-engineering, performance measurement or the 'virtual' corporation?

The most enduring theories of today are also likely to be about 'people issues'; ideas that redefine our approach to human aspirations in the workplace, to the development of talent, trust, creativity and loyalty, without which a business is nothing but hardware, software and the fickleness of markets. If one were to place a bet on the survival of recent management theories, the safe money is likely to be on the learning organization, if only because it is all about the interdependence of the individual and the whole; it is capable of infinite interpretations and (cynically), it is virtually impossible to disprove as the template for tomorrow's company.

1

JOHN ADAIR

(b. 1934)

Action-Centred Leadership : how task, team and individual overlap

Pioneering British thinker in the theory and practice of leadership, and the first to occupy a chair in leadership studies in the UK (at the University of Surrey, 1979–1983). Since 1991 he has been visiting professor in leadership studies at the University of Exeter, which established the world's first diploma and master's degree in leadership in 1993. A centre for leadership studies was set up at Exeter in 1997.

Cambridge graduate Adair, whose quiet and business-like demeanour is belied by a colourful career including service in a Bedouin regiment under Glubb Pasha; working as a deckhand on an Arctic trawler; and lecturing at the Royal Military Academy, Sandhurst, has written more than 25 books on leadership and management development. He now works as an international management consultant and runs his own publishing company.

Before his appointment to the leadership chair at Surrey, Adair was visiting fellow at the Oxford Centre for Management Studies and assistant director of The Industrial Society, where he headed the leadership department.

Adair believes his contribution to management thinking is threefold. He can claim to have been the first to demonstrate that people can be trained for leadership as a transferable skill rather than a matter of inborn aptitude. Second, he has helped alter the concept of management

1

to include the larger element of leadership, with which he associated the neighbouring skills of decision-making, communication, and ability to manage time. Finally, he has defined leadership in terms of three overlapping circles – Task, Team and Individual – distilled into his teaching concept, Action-Centred Leadership (ACL).

Without undue modesty, Adair suggests that the ACL model is 'emerging in management studies, in effect, as something akin to Einstein's General Theory of Relativity.' It does, he maintains, 'identify the main forces at work in working groups and organizations, and it charts . . . their main interrelationships with a degree of predictive accuracy.'

ACL encompasses much of the teaching on individual human needs first charted by Abraham Maslow (qv) and Frederick Herzberg (qv). It was developed by Adair first at Sandhurst and later at The Industrial Society.

Adair's best-known books on leadership are *Effective Leadership*, *Not Bosses But Leaders* and *Great Leaders*, a study of leadership qualities in historical figures. He claims his 'mission' is to be 'in the forefront of long-term management thinking' and to integrate management concepts to better effect.

John Adair goes to etymological roots to explain the crucial difference between 'leading' and 'managing'. In an interview in *Director* magazine (November 1988), he explained it neatly:

> Leadership is about a sense of direction. The word 'lead' comes from an Anglo-Saxon word, common to north European languages, which means a road, a way, the path of a ship at sea. It's knowing what the next step is . . . . Managing is a different image. It's from the Latin manus, a hand. It's handling a sword, a ship, a horse. It tends to be closely linked with the idea of machines. Managing had its origins in the 19th century with engineers and

accountants coming in to run entrepreneurial outfits. They tended to think of them as systems.

But there are valuable ingredients in the concept of management that are not present in leadership. Managing is very strong on the idea of controlling, particularly financial control, and administration. Leaders are not necessarily good at administration or managing resources.

What leaders are – or should be – good at, he elaborated in the same interview, is inspiring others. 'That's tied in with the leader's own enthusiasm and commitment and with the ability to communicate and share that enthusiasm with others and to enthuse them. It's not quite the same as motivation, which is something that's learned about in the business schools, a rather mechanical thing.

'And leadership is about teamwork, creating teams. Teams tend to have leaders, leaders tend to create teams.

'Finally, you can be appointed a manager, but you're not a leader until your appointment is "ratified" in the hearts and minds of those who work for you. There's got to be a degree of acceptance of you by followers that is not necessary if you're just holding an appointment.'

The ethos of the team is at the heart of Adair's leadership theories and his Action-Centred Leadership model. He believes that working groups share three areas of common needs: the need to accomplish a common task, the need to be maintained as a cohesive social unit or team, and the sum of the group's individual needs. These form his overlapping 'three-circle model': failure in one area affects the other two. For example, failure to achieve the task (or lack of a task altogether) will both disrupt the sense of teamship and lower the level of individual satisfaction. The approach can best be understood by drawing three interlocking circles labelled Task, Team and Individual and placing a coin over any one of them. Segments of the other two are immediately blotted out. The overlapping circles, maintains Adair, illustrate 'the essential unity of leadership; a single action can be multi-functional in that it touches all areas.'

In *Understanding Motivation* (1990), Adair lists the functions of leadership as originally worked out at Sandhurst:

- Planning (seeking all available information; defining group tasks or goals; making a workable plan)
- Initiating (briefing the group; allocating tasks; setting group standards)
- Controlling (maintaining group standards; ensuring progress towards objectives; 'prodding' actions and decisions)
- Supporting (expressing acceptance of individual contributions; encouraging and disciplining; creating team spirit; relieving tension with humour; reconciling disagreements)
- Informing (clarifying task and plan; keeping group informed; receiving information from the group; summarizing ideas and suggestions)
- Evaluating (checking feasibility of ideas; testing consequences; evaluating group performance; helping group to evaluate itself)

The functions of leadership are a key element in Adair's integrated ACL theory, in which the three-circle model plays a central role without being the whole concept. The originality of ACL, he points out, lies not in its parts – 'none of which were actually brought into their first existence by me' – but in their integration into a whole and the application of that whole to training.

'By being brought into a new relation with one another, those parts have undergone varying degrees of transformation, which is inevitable in any creative work.'

Among the constituents borrowed and re-evaluated from earlier gurus are Maslow's 'hierarchy of needs' model and Henri Fayol's classic definitions of management functions. In *Understanding Motivation*, Adair also expounds his 'Fifty-Fifty Rule,' a variation on the Pareto Principle, in which he contends that half an individual's motivation comes from within himself or herself, the other half from external factors, including leadership. This theory contradicts most of the motivation gurus, led by Maslow and Herzberg, who stressed that motivation lies pre-eminently within the individual.

Adair has applied his Fifty-Fifty Rule in other contexts,

for example in *Effective Teambuilding* (Gower, 1986), where he suggests that 50 per cent of success depends on the team and 50 per cent on the leader. The Fifty-Fifty Rule has the benefit, he says, of challenging each party to get its performance right before criticizing the quality or contribution of the other. 'It is the ultimate cure for the "Us and Them" disease of organizations.'

KEY WRITINGS

Adair, J. (1983) *Effective Leadership*, Aldershot: Gower.
Adair, J. (1986) *Effective Teambuilding*, Aldershot: Gower.
Adair, J. (1988) *Not Bosses But Leaders*, Guildford: Talbot Adair Press.
Adair, J. (1988) *Developing Leaders*, Guildford: Talbot Adair Press.
Adair, J. (1989) *Great Leaders*, Guildford: Talbot Adair Press.
Adair, J. (1990) *Understanding Motivation*, Guildford: Talbot Adair Press.
Adair, J. (1996) *Effective Leadership Masterclass*, London: Pan.
Adair, J. (1997) *Effective Communication*, London: Pan.
Adair, J. (1997) *Effective Innovation*, London: Pan.
Adair, J. (1998) Thomas, Neil (ed.) *The John Adair Management and Leadership Handbook*, London: Thorogood.

2

H. IGOR ANSOFF

(b. 1918)

The theory and practice of strategic planning

Russian-born pioneer of strategic management and corporate planning, whose 1965 book *Corporate Strategy* was described by Henry Mintzberg as 'the most elaborate model of strategic planning in the literature.' Professor Bernard Taylor of Henley Management College, a leading British authority on strategic planning, describes Ansoff as 'the guru's guru' in the field, which he effectively founded in 1963, the year he left Lockheed to teach strategy at Carnegie Institute of Technology. Until that time, Taylor recalls, 'business policy was regarded as a "capstone course" in general management which had no theory to speak of and therefore must be taught entirely by the case method.'

From *Corporate Strategy* (recently republished as *The New Corporate Strategy*), onwards, Ansoff's major books have been milestones in the development of strategic management: *Business Strategy* (1969), *From Strategic Planning to Strategic Management* (1976), *Strategic Management* (1979) and *Implanting Strategic Management* (1984, 1990). The last two, representing a shift from a focus on strategy to the 'bottom line' success of strategic behaviour, have consolidated his leadership in a field that remained underrated, in the UK at least, until the mid-1980s.

Born in Vladivostock of a Russian mother and an

American diplomat father, Ansoff spent his first 16 years in newly Sovietized Russia. The family then returned to New York, where Ansoff studied mechanical engineering and physics. After service in World War II he took a doctorate in applied mathematics under a government sponsorship scheme for ex-servicemen.

In 1948 Ansoff joined the Rand Foundation, an influential think-tank of the postwar years specializing in military problems. Here he worked on strategic problems of NATO, and the methodology he developed for strategic problem-solving was later to prove a powerful influence on his development of theory and practical technology for business.

Joining the Lockheed aerospace company as a long-range planner gave him a practical outlet when he was appointed to be responsible for Lockheed's diversification. He has said that this job gave him the opportunity to learn how business works and how to identify the key variables and relationships in complex problems. He was promoted to vice-president and general manager in Lockheed Electronics Company where he was faced with the human traumas involved in reducing a division with 17 high technology businesses down to three, requiring the layoff of 100 engineers. Thus he learned at first hand the difficult part of management, which is managing other people's lives.

Managing a large corporation did not, however, fulfil Ansoff's own long-term career strategy. He became a professor at Carnegie School of Industrial Administration, and shortly after joining Carnegie published his seminal *Corporate Strategy*.

His next move was to become founding dean of the Graduate School of Management at Vanderbilt University in Nashville, Tennessee, where he created a pioneering new business school, based on the concept of strategic management, to train 'change agents.'

Although *Corporate Strategy* received worldwide acceptance, the prescription for strategic planning contained in the book produced mixed results in practice. In some firms it produced significant improvement in performance and became a way of life, but in many others, strategic planning became a phenomenon which Ansoff called 'paralysis by analysis.'

Ansoff decided to find an explanation of this anomaly, a decision which led to 20 years of theoretical and empirical research on successful strategic behaviours. An early step was a four-year research study of success and failure of mergers and acquisitions strategies, the outcome of which was *Acquisition Behaviour of US Manufacturing Firms 1946–1965*, published in 1971. In the following year Ansoff published an article, 'The Concept of Strategic Management', which argued that explanation of the planning failure must be sought through studying the firm's overall process of strategic management and not just the planning component. Ansoff organized the first international multidisciplinary conference on strategic management, sponsored by IBM and General Electric, at Vanderbilt in 1973. An outcome of this conference was *From Strategic Planning to Strategic Management*, published in 1974.

Ansoff spent the next six years at the Brussels-based European Institute of Advanced Studies in Management, where he led a number of pan-European projects on strategic management and societal strategy and continued his research on strategic management, in particular on the identification of the kinds of strategic behaviour that lead to success in organizations in turbulent environments.

Out of this research came *Strategic Management* (1979), which offered a comprehensive theory of strategic behaviour, and *Implanting Strategic Management* (1984, 1990), which presents a comprehensive practical approach to optimizing strategic behaviour.

Ansoff returned to the US in 1983 to become Distinguished Professor of Strategic Management at US International University, where he created masters' and doctoral level programmes in strategic management. He also formed his own consultancy in San Diego, California.

Igor Ansoff's *Corporate Strategy*, as the author wrote in his preface, seeks 'to develop a practically useful series of concepts and procedures which managers can use to manage . . . a practical method for strategic decision-making within a business firm.'

The book accomplishes this with a methodology of processes and checklists so detailed and rigorous that the former ICI chairman, Sir John Harvey-Jones, introducing the 1986 edition in Sidgwick and Jackson's Library of Management Classics, observed that, using it, 'superficially at least, the corporate strategy could be drawn up by an unintelligent computer . . . .' Harvey-Jones went on to rank the book as 'one of the best business books of all time.'

Professor Bernard Taylor of Henley Management College describes it as 'a brilliant, original contribution, and still an essential introduction to the concept of strategy.' Since the 1970s, however, Ansoff has moved away from the prescriptive approach of the book, which, according to a leading member of Britain's Strategic Planning Society, tended to be interpreted by some of Ansoff's followers in too deterministic a manner ('he preached rigour, not rigidity'). Ansoff's most recent works focus on the necessity of building flexibility and adaptation to change into the planning process.

Corporate Strategy begins by analysing the three main types of decision-making – strategic, administrative and operating – and how they interact. It then explains the specific questions addressed in the strategic category:

• What are the firm's objectives and goals?
• Should the firm seek to diversify, in what areas and how vigorously?
• How should the firm develop and exploit its present product-market position?

Ansoff explains that most strategic decisions have to be made within the practical framework of a limited total resource, involving a choice of alternative commitments among resources. Thus, emphasis on current business activity will preclude diversification; over-emphasis on diversification will lead to neglect of present products. 'The object is to produce a resource-allocation pattern which will offer the best potential for meeting the firm's objectives.'

Ansoff next examines how those objectives, both economic and social, can be defined by individual firms according to their own circumstances; moves on to devise a practical method of setting objectives within varying time horizons and of building in enough flexibility to cope with unforeseen calamities or catastrophic change.

'Objectives,' Ansoff writes, 'are a management tool with many potential uses. In the operating problem they can be used for establishing performance standards and objectives for all organizational levels, for appraisal of performance, and for control decisions. In the administrative problem they can be used to diagnose deficiencies in the organizational structure. In our main area of interest, the strategic problem, objectives are used as yardsticks for decisions on changes, deletions and additions to the firm's product-market posture.'

The book then moves into denser thickets of analysis, evolving its own mathematical formulae to demonstrate the meaning of synergy as a component in strategy, applied to acquisitions, start-ups and diversifications. Ansoff follows this by developing a 'concept of strategy' from which a firm can (1) identify the business it should be in, (2) use specific guidelines to search for strategic opportunities and (3) be given decision rules to narrow that selection process down to the most attractive options.

Ansoff preceded Harvard's Michael Porter (qv) by nearly two decades in identifying 'competitive advantage' as a key element in strategic planning. He observed that identifying a competitive advantage requires 'uncommon skills in anticipating trends' to ensure really successful results, and that, because of the need for knowledge of the industries involved, the concentric form of diversification (linked related products and markets) is likely to be more successful than conglomerate diversification.

Corporate Strategy concludes by analysing the pros and cons of 'make or buy' new product-markets, e.g. whether to plump for organic growth or acquisition.

In summary, *Corporate Strategy* provides both the concepts

and practice of strategic decision-making, starting with the philosophical issues that underlie company objectives and progressing to the point at which the firm commits itself to a specific product-market strategy. It finally develops a procedure for appraising and monitoring a strategic project and explains how strategy fits as a management tool into the overall periodic planning process of a firm.

Ansoff's work in Brussels on strategic behaviour patterns and their results on organizations, which was embodied in his theoretical book *Strategic Management*, has been described by him as 'the most important phase of my intellectual development . . . I begged, borrowed and stole concepts and theoretical insights from psychology, sociology and political science. And I attempted to integrate them into a holistic explanation of strategic behaviour.' The centrepiece of the theory presented in that book was the Strategic Success Hypothesis.

While in Brussels he also wrote a series of three important papers ('Strategic Issue Management' [1980], 'Managing Strategic Surprise by Response to Weak Signals' [1976] and 'Dispersal Positioning in Strategic Portfolio Analysis' [with Kirsch and Roventa, 1980]). These developed a set of practical methods for adapting a firm to fast-changing and unpredictable threats and opportunities.

Implanting Strategic Management, first published in 1984 and updated in 1990, translated the theoretical concepts of the 1979 book into practical 'how to do it' technology. It represents the distillation of Ansoff's 35 years' experience in management (as manager, teacher and consultant) and a culmination of his 20 years' search for a comprehensive explanation of why the original strategic planning failed to work.

Ansoff explains that since the 1960s his thinking developed along three parallel paths: enlargement of his scientific perspective from unidisciplinary to multidisciplinary; the search for a theoretical explanation of strategic behaviour, and development of practical technology for strategic management in turbulent environments.

Implanting Strategic Management is built on the 'strategic success formula' (a practical translation of the strategic success hypothesis), which states that a firm's performance is

11

optimized when its external strategy and internal capability are both matched to the turbulence of the firm's external environment.

The book reports that the strategic success formula has been 'empirically validated' in eight countries around the world, in different industries and in banks.

Implanting Strategic Management represents the most comprehensive exposition of concepts and practical techniques current in strategic management, and recommends processes for creating a dual system within a firm which can both manage strategic change and the daily profit-making activities.

Since his return to the US in 1983, Ansoff has been developing further his work on strategic behaviour, with particular emphasis on patterns that lead to success – most crucially, the ability to manage strategic responses to a turbulent external environment – and on helping firms to behave successfully in strategic terms. He claims that the strategic success formula demonstrates that the days of simple, universal management prescriptions are over, and that each organization must work out its own best solution, whose complexity is neither higher nor lower than the complexity of the firm's environment. Ansoff offers *Implanting Strategic Management* as a tool for finding this solution.

Professor Taylor says Ansoff's work has 'educated and enthused a whole generation of practitioners, consultants and academics in the USA and around the world.' Throughout his distinguished academic career, 'he has kept his contact with practice, working with top management teams in leading multinational companies – always bringing new and original ideas, expressed with energy and enthusiasm.'

KEY WRITINGS

Ansoff, H. I. (1965) *Corporate Strategy*, New York: McGraw Hill; (1986) London: Sidgwick and Jackson.
Ansoff, H. I. (1969) *Business Strategy*, London: Penguin

Books.

Ansoff, H. I. (1971) *Behavior of US Manufacturing Firms 1946–65* (with R. J. Brandenburg, F. E. Portner, H. R. Radosevich), Nashville: Vanderbilt University Press.

Ansoff, H. I. (1976) *From Strategic Planning to Strategic Management* (with R. Hays, R. Declerck), New York and London: John Wiley and Sons.

Ansoff, H. I. (1979) *Strategic Management*, London: Macmillan.

Ansoff, H. I. (1984, 1990) *Implanting Strategic Management*, New Jersey: Prentice-Hall.

3
CHRIS ARGYRIS
(b. 1923)

Developing individual potential within the organization; single and double-loop learning

US organizational psychologist whose special area is the personal development of individuals within organizations, and the defence mechanisms that managers often unwittingly use to resist change.

One of the squadron of eminent management thinkers associated with Harvard University, he has been James Bryant Conant Professor of Educational and Organizational Behaviour there since 1971. Before that he was Professor of Industrial Administration at rival Yale University.

Argyris has also worked as a consultant in industry, notably for IBM, Shell and Du Pont, as well as for various departments of the US government and for governments in Europe. He is a full board member of the UK consultancy Monitor, which Michael Porter (qv) helped to found.

Peter Drucker has called organization theorists like Argyris 'romantics' for hoping that by encouraging the principle of participation they can disprove the anarchist assertion that 'organization is alienation.'

Drucker himself has no such ideals. 'Authority is an essential dimension of work,' he wrote in *Management: Tasks, Responsibilities, Practices* (1973). 'It has little or nothing to do with ownership of the means of production, democracy at the workplace, worker representation or any other way of structuring the "system". It is inherent in the fact of organization.'

Argyris starts from the premise that each individual has a potential that can be developed – or stultified – by the organization and the particular group circumstances in which he or she works. Developing a person's full potential should be to the benefit of both the individual and the organization, his argument runs, but managers and even peer groups within the organization often lack the 'interpersonal confidence' to allow this to flourish. Managers in particular, he warns, may develop defensive mechanisms to protect their control over others.

In an article for *Harvard Business Review* in which Argyris studied six companies and observed 265 decision-making meetings, he concluded that executive behaviour often creates an atmosphere of distrust and inflexibility, despite the fact that the executives involved genuinely believe trust and innovation to be crucial to good decision-making.

Argyris observed that such discrepancies were not restricted to business organizations: he had obtained similar patterns of behaviour from leaders in education, research, the church, trade unions and government.

His solution was for executives to try asking important 'feedback' questions, at quiet and non-risky times when the pressure was off, discussing tapes of their own meetings and actively entering a learning process about their own behaviour and that of their group.

He identified three basic values that affected his study groups:

- 'The significant human relationships are the ones which have to do with achieving the organization's objective.' In other words, executives concentrated their efforts on 'getting the job done', often using this as an excuse to avoid probing into workers' interpersonal factors and how groups were getting on together.

- 'Cognitive rationality is to be emphasized; feelings and emotions are to be played down.' Thus interpersonal relations are viewed as irrelevant, not real work.
- 'Human relationships are most effectively influenced through unilateral direction, coercion and control, as well as by rewards and penalties that sanction all three values.' Direction and control are accepted, Argyris found, as an inevitable, unquestioned part of the managerial chain of command.

The whole suppressed awareness of what senior management was doing was summed up by Argyris: 'During the study of the decision-making processes of the president and the nine vice-presidents of a firm with nearly 3,000 employees, I concluded that the members unknowingly behaved in such a way as not to encourage risk-taking, openness, expression of feelings and cohesive, trusting relationships.'

But in later interviews, the executives claimed that negative feelings were not expressed because 'we trust each other and respect each other.' The reasons why issues of conflict were ignored at meetings included such explanations as: 'we should not air our dirty linen in front of people who may come in to make a presentation,' and 'when people are emotional, they are not rational.'

A similar pattern of misinterpreted signals emerged from studies of executives' relationships with middle managers, most of the latter feeling that they did not know where they stood with their bosses and that conflicts were very rarely tackled.

'One key to group and organizational effectiveness is to get this knowledge (that a group was decaying) out into the open and to discuss it thoroughly. The human "motors" of the group and the organization have to be checked periodically, just as does the motor of an automobile. Without proper maintenance, all will fail.' (*Harvard Business Review*: 'Interpersonal Barriers to Decision-Making').

Argyris worked with Donald A. Schon on examining how organizations cope with the contradictory goals of maintaining a stable status quo and adapting to change

(*Organizational Learning: A Theory of Action Perspective*). How, for example, do members of an organization reconcile such opposing messages in their culture as: take initiatives but keep to the rules; think ahead but remember that pay is linked to present performance; cooperate with others but be ready to compete with them?

Argyris and Schon developed what they call Model I to demonstrate how managers resolve these contradictions. What they do is to concentrate on setting goals as an individual; on being as self-contained as possible; on keeping negative feelings to themselves and on discouraging others from speaking their minds about matters that worry them. In this way they hope to protect their own positions and to deflect issues that could build up a head of steam in other people.

The primary aim of Model I managers is to defend themselves and their positions from change while imposing change where necessary on others. Where they fail, however, is in creating mistrust and repression. The process is self-perpetuating because they learn nothing except the importance of conforming. This is described by Argyris as 'single-loop' learning. The prescription he and Schon worked out for Model II management proposes 'double-loop' learning, which takes an opposite course: here the manager acts on information (once assured that it is valid), invites free discussion and choice and is prepared to change. Double-loop learning involves learning from others rather than from one's own self-perpetuating experience.

To switch managers from Model I to Model II thinking, Argyris advises a training programme for managers using interpersonal consultants.

He is fully aware of the difficulties involved in making the change. In *Strategy, Change and Defensive Routines*, he writes: 'Top management believes that to change defensive routines is the equivalent of changing the world, a belief that I share with them. They conclude that the most realistic solution is to bypass them . . . .'

Argyris explains that organizations can perform well in spite of defensive routines operating within them: indeed, defensive managers are usually loyal, hard-working and dedicated. The best advice in tackling defensive routines, says Argyris, is 'to move slowly and iteratively. Let the organization learn from each experiment so it can make the next one even more successful and build up organizational intelligence on these change processes that can be disseminated throughout the organization.'

Defensive routines are one strong reason why changing the existing culture in organizations rarely lasts, however. In Argyris' view, 'defensive routines pollute the system and undermine it the same way air pollution undermines our lives.'

KEY WRITINGS

Argyris, C. (1957) *Personality and Organization*, New York: Harper and Row.

Argyris, C. (1965) *Organization and Innovation*, Toronto: Irwin.

Argyris, C. and Schon, D. A. (1978) *Organizational Learning: A Theory of Action Perspective*, Wokingham: Addison-Wesley.

Argyris, C. (1985) *Strategy, Change and Defensive Routines*, London: Pitman.

Argyris, C. (1991) 'Teaching Smart People How to Learn', Cambridge, Mass.: *Harvard Business Review* (May/June).

Argyris, C. (1994) 'Good Communication That Blocks Learning', Cambridge, Mass.: *Harvard Business Review* (July/Aug).

4

CHESTER BARNARD

(1886–1961)

Managing the values of the organization

New England-born Chester Barnard was a rarity among management gurus in being a full-time business executive. He spent 40 years with the Bell Telephone Company and eventually became president of New Jersey Bell.

Barnard was one of the first to study the process of decision-making in organizations, the relationships between formal and informal organizations, and the role and function of the executive. His 1938 book *The Functions of the Executive* exerted tremendous influence in its time: in it, he identified what we now call 'Organization Man,' stating that 'the most important single contribution required of the executive, certainly the most universal qualification, is loyalty, domination by the organization personality.'

Barnard saw business organizations as more effective instruments of social progress than either church or state, partly because they were driven by the cooperation of individuals working to a common purpose rather than by authority.

Barnard's work also encompassed pioneering thinking on the nature of leadership, upon which others have built, and on corporate culture and value-shaping, a good 30 years before the rest of the management world woke up to their importance. The real role of the chief executive, he suggested, was to manage the values of the organization, as well as to secure employee commitment. Peters and Waterman in their *In Search of Excellence* paid tribute to Barnard's work as 'probably the first balanced treatment of the management process.'

In the late 1930s, the work of Chester Barnard and Elton Mayo challenged the long-established theories of Max Weber (qv), who defined (and admired) the organization as bureaucracy, and F. W. Taylor (qv), who believed that management could be made an exact science, capable of being applied by a set of rules.

Barnard recognized that organizations are made up of individual human beings with individual motivations, and that every large formal organization carries within it a host of smaller, less formal groupings whose goals need to be harnessed to those of the parent body. This linkage Barnard saw as the responsibility of management. He made an important distinction between management effectiveness and management efficiency, and argued that to be effective, an organization's purpose or goals must be accepted by all the contributors to its system of effort. The willingness of all concerned to cooperate in a common purpose was essential, Barnard considered, to an organization's survival.

For a businessman of his time, Barnard was remarkably percipient in the message he constantly reiterated: that authority in an organization only exists insofar as the people in that organization are willing to accept it. Hence his emphasis on the value of communications, and his three basic principles for ensuring their effectiveness:

- Everyone should know what the channels of communication are
- Everyone should have access to a formal channel of communication
- Lines of communication should be as short and direct as possible

The functions of managers, Barnard believed, were to establish and manage that system of communications; to motivate employees towards the organization's goals, and to formulate those goals in a clearly communicable way. *In Search of Excellence* pinpoints Barnard's contribution to the theory of corporate culture (then barely in its infancy) and the role of the executive within it. 'Barnard was . . . the first (we know of) to talk about the primary role of the chief executive as the shaper and manager of shared values in an organization,' wrote Peters and Waterman.

Barnard's emphasis on managing the corporate whole was still an unusual concept at the time Peters and Waterman were writing in the early 1980s. He was alone among his contemporaries in sensing 'the unconventional and critical role of executives in making it all happen,' the *Excellence* authors observed. In the preface to *The Functions of the Executive*, Barnard stated that his primary aim was to provide a comprehensive theory of cooperative behaviour in formal organizations.

Barnard's contribution to leadership theory is bound up with this concept of the good manager as value shaper. He contrasted this concept with that of the authoritarian, manipulative manager working strictly on a system of rewards and short-term efficiency. But his theories, as Peters and Waterman pointed out, lay virtually dormant for 30 years while most management thinking concentrated on structure and its relation to postwar growth.

The fact that his vision of an organization is essentially one of desired equilibrium – a state sought by all leading management theorists until comparatively recently – has led to a critical reassessment by those gurus like Richard Pascale (qv) of *Managing on the Edge*, who believe that the vital organization of today must welcome change, discontinuity and even conflict within itself, and manage those things creatively. Pascale points out that Barnard advocates 'coherence among such elements as values, informal social networks, formal systems and purposes. The better they are orchestrated, the better the organization performs.'

Some of Barnard's disciples, notably Jay Lorsch of Harvard, have filled this gap by evolving 'contingency theory'. But on the whole, Barnard's theories are deemed to be as relevant today as they were in the late 1930s.

Despite this, his work is largely neglected, perhaps because some of his books, especially *The Functions of the Executive*, are written in a fairly impenetrable style. Peters and Waterman call it 'virtually unreadable,' but they have no doubt that it remains a monument in management theory.

KEY WRITINGS

Barnard, C. (1938) *The Functions of the Executive*, Cambridge, Mass.: Harvard University Press.
Barnard, C. (1948) *Organization and Management*, Cambridge, Mass.: Harvard University Press.

5

MEREDITH BELBIN

(b. 1926)

Complementary roles in team-building

Ex-psychologist and training expert whose system of selecting and building teams out of complementing and balancing the strengths and 'allowable weaknesses' of individuals has become an industry standard.

A rangy, energetic man still fizzing with ideas in his early seventies, Belbin first studied classics at Clare College, Cambridge, then switched in his final year to experimental psychology. His first – and abiding – interest in training was in the development and employment of older workers; his MA and PhD in 1952 were in gerontology, and later he worked as a consultant for OECD in Paris developing the 'guided discovery' method of enabling older workers to learn new skills. It was put into operation in OECD-sponsored projects in the UK, US, Austria and Sweden and described in a book called *Problems in Adult Retraining* (1972), written with his wife, Eunice.

The Belbin team selection system grew out of a research programme with Henley Management College in 1967 into the effectiveness of management teams. Finding that the more complementary their contributions or roles, the better the team performed, Belbin developed psychometric tests to assess the contributions which each individual could make. These tests are also now widely used in the selection of senior personnel.

Belbin's two key books in this field are *Management Teams: Why They Succeed or Fail* (1981), described by the *Financial Times* as one of the top 50 business books of all time, and *Team Roles at Work* (1993). The first explains the evolution of Belbin's 'team role' theory, based on findings that 'imperfect people can make perfect teams' through balancing weaknesses with strengths in the team makeup. The second offers a methodology for combining independent observer assessments with self-assessments. Properly applied, the system shows that effective people have learned to project themselves accurately and the way they see themselves corresponds with others' perceptions. The wider the gap between the two, the less effective people are in teams.

Belbin's energy and range of interests remains phenomenal. As well as his family-run consultancy BelBin Associates in Cambridge, he lectures by invitation in the UK and overseas, and is working with Brathay Hall Trust in the Lake District on various training programmes including a course for 'the elite prospective entrepreneur.' Like Henry Mintzberg (qv), he believes that business schools fail to teach the realities of management.

The onetime classical scholar is still fascinated by the workings of ancient societies and has recently extended his studies of collective organizations to the insect world. In *The Coming Shape of Organizations* (1996), he looks at what we can learn from ants, termites and bees and argues that, whereas the intellect of *homo sapiens* works most brilliantly in individuals, that of insect societies grows in power collectively.

Belbin himself describes his myriad research projects as having a unifying thread of an 'experimental approach to problems in business and social affairs, the creation of new conceptual models and the development of the means by which they can be delivered.' His style of working is 'empirical and operational,' and he describes the core of what he does as: 'Diversity is in our genes. It's how to capture this diversity in groups and use it to best advantage.'

Meredith Belbin's system of psychometric testing for the selection of senior staff and the construction of effective management teams has become such an integral tool of the human resources business that it is commonly referred to simply by its inventor's surname, as in, 'We use Belbin in our recruitment.'

Yet the recent rediscovery of the virtues of self-managed teams (pioneered by Douglas MacGregor, qv, in the late 1950s) has not, curiously, caused the world to beat a bigger path to his door. Belbin thinks this is because self-managed teams tend to be approached in the wrong way; less genuine empowerment than a convenient way for managers to shift responsibility.

While working for the Industrial Training Unit at University College, London, in 1967, he was invited to Henley Management College to study competing 'company' teams on a computer-based business game called Executive Management Effectiveness that formed part of a management course. He found very different patterns of effectiveness, linked to the behaviour patterns of team members and the ways in which each contributed to the whole.

Complementary contributions produced better results than competing contributions and one key finding was that certain strengths in individuals were often associated with what Belbin termed 'allowable weaknesses.' Such weaknesses were not detrimental to effective teamwork because they could be underpinned by the strengths of others. Sharing this knowledge helped to build effectiveness, along with the realization that 'imperfect people can make perfect teams.'

Management Teams: Why They Succeed or Fail sets out the eight main roles which contribute to the ideal team – company worker, chairman, shaper, plant, resource investigator, monitor-evaluator, team worker and completer-finisher. Their basic characteristics are defined as:

Company worker: conservative, dutiful, predictable, with organizing ability, practical common sense, hardworking. Allowable weakness: lack of flexibility, unresponsiveness to unproven ideas.

Chairman: calm, self-confident, controlled, with a capacity for treating all potential contributors on their merits and a strong sense of objectives. Allowable weakness: ordinary intellect and creative ability.

Shaper: highly strung, outgoing, dynamic, with drive and a readiness to challenge inertia, ineffectiveness, complacency or self-deception. Allowable weakness: prone to provocation, irritation, impatience.

Plant: individualistic, serious, unorthodox, with genius, imagination, intellect, knowledge. Allowable weakness: up in the clouds, inclined to disregard practical details or protocol.

Resource investigator: extroverted, enthusiastic, curious, communicative, with a capacity for contacting people and exploring anything new. An ability to respond to challenge. Allowable weakness: liable to lose interest once the initial fascination has passed.

Monitor–evaluator: sober, unemotional, prudent, with judgement, discretion, hard-headedness. Allowable weakness: lacks inspiration or the ability to motivate others.

Team worker: socially orientated, rather mild, sensitive, with an ability to respond to people and situations, and to promote team spirit. Allowable weakness: indecisiveness at moments of crisis.

Completer–finisher: painstaking, orderly, conscientious, anxious, with a capacity for follow-through. Perfectionism. Allowable weakness: a tendency to worry about small things, a reluctance to let go.

Characteristics were assessed in two ways: through questionnaires completed by the participants themselves and through outside observations by course members who were more interested in watching than in participating. There were seven observed categories of contributory behaviour: asking, informing, proposing, opposing, delegating, building and commenting.

The book went on to analyse the designing and leading of teams, ideal team sizes and how to foster creativity in a team. Interestingly, one type of 'company' team participating at Henley, composed of exceptionally clever individuals, actually finished last, and continued to perform poorly through repeated experiments. Nicknamed 'Apollo' companies, they were hard to manage, prone to destructive debate and showed difficulties in decision-making. Belbin concluded that 'high critical faculties bring destructive tendencies to the fore.'

In his follow-up book, *Team Roles at Work*, Belbin says: 'A team is not a bunch of people with job titles, but a congregation of individuals, each of whom has a role that is understood by other members . . . Members of teams seek out certain roles and they perform most effectively in the ones that are most natural to them.'

Team Roles at Work further explores the original role concepts and sets out the 'construct' theory on which Belbin's team selection and building process works. The key to this is the integration of self-perception and perception by outside observers. When the two coincide, the result is an effective team performer: the wider the gap, the greater the chance of failure. For the computer-based management programme which integrates the feedback data, Belbin and his son and partner Nigel have developed software that filters and weights information fed into it so that it cannot be deceived or corrupted by false or misleading data. *Team Roles at Work* is described by Belbin as 'a halfway house to understanding the Belbin method,' though he says it is often applied simplistically.

Belbin's belief in the value of teams extends to his views on leadership and chimes with the latest thinking of Warren Bennis (qv) on 'Great Groups.' Strategic leadership, Belbin asserts, is 'much safer vested in small strategic teams rather than in a single individual.'

His 1996 book *The Coming Shape of Organizations* examines how insect societies can form models for the large-scale human organization to reinvent itself as a series of small teams. He describes the concept in this way: 'Small interacting teams act without interference and rely on their superior capacity for generating and acting on complex information. They have no "appeal" systems, so cannot be disempowered . . . Concurrent teams, comprising small competing teams, produce better results in tackling complex problems than one large conferring group headed by a leader.'

27

'A model of the future organization, and for career progression, is the progression helix. People have personal jobs but are also invited into teams. An internal labour market competes for the best team members and one person may be invited into positions that would otherwise be perceived as belonging to different parts of the hierarchy.'

KEY WRITINGS

Belbin, M. (1981) *Management Teams: Why They Succeed or Fail*, Oxford: Butterworth Heinemann.
Belbin, M. (1993) T*eam Roles at Work*, Oxford: Butterworth Heinemann.
Belbin, M. (1996) *The Coming Shape of Organizations*, Oxford: Butterworth Heinemann.
Belbin, M. (1997) *Changing the Way We Work*, Oxford: Butterworth Heinemann.

Video films: Building the Perfect Team (Video Arts)
Selecting the Perfect Team (Video Arts)

6
WARREN BENNIS

(b. 1925)

'Managers do things right. Leaders do the right thing'

New York-born industrial psychologist and adviser to four US presidents, best known as a guru of leadership theory, though his earlier work was concerned with organizational development. He is famous for his aphorism: 'Managers do things right. Leaders do the right thing.'

Like Abraham Maslow (qv) and Britain's Charles Handy (qv), Bennis was strongly influenced while at MIT's Sloan School of Management by Douglas McGregor (qv) and his 'Theory X and Theory Y'. Like Maslow, he attempted to put Theory Y into action in a practical management setting – upgrading the run-down University of Buffalo in the late 1960s – and found that it would not work without a stiffening framework of structure, direction and controls.

His vision of the organization of the future in *The Temporary Society* (1968) identified the need for 'adhocracy' (free-moving project teams) – a principle espoused by Alvin Toffler in *Future Shock*, by Henry Mintzberg (qv) and most recently by Robert H. Waterman Jr.

From 1971 to 1977 Bennis was president of the University of Cincinnati, but he has worked internationally in France, Switzerland and India. He is now Distinguished Professor of Business Administration and founder of the Leadership Institute at the University of Southern California in San Diego.

29

In the best-selling *Leaders: The Strategies for Taking Charge*, which he wrote in 1985 with Burt Nanus and which established his reputation as a world authority on leadership, Bennis studied 90 individuals in different sections of US society, including astronaut Neil Armstrong, sports coaches and orchestra conductors as well as businessmen, and identified four factors or 'competencies' common to all – the ability to manage attention, meaning, trust and self.

Since the mid-1980s he has been moving away from the study of the leader as heroic individual towards that of group leadership, believing that the former model no longer works in today's much-altered organizations, except where deep culture change is required. In his 1997 work, *Organizing Genius*, he analyses what he calls 'Great Groups' – dynamic and dedicated teams for whom the project is all, from Walt Disney Studios to the scientists of the Manhattan Project who built the first atomic bomb – and reformulates his earlier four competencies into four 'new rules' of leadership. Without exception, he says, leaders of such groups:

- Provide direction and meaning, a sense of purpose
- Generate and sustain trust, creating authentic relationships
- Display a bias towards action, risk-taking and curiosity
- Are purveyors of hope, optimism and a psychological resilience that expects success

Bennis' own personal first encounter with such qualities came in 1944, when he was serving in the US army in Europe as a 19-year-old second lieutenant. His company commander, one Captain Bessinger, was 'the kind of leader you read about in the Bible.' He listened to his men, taught them the skills of survival and conveyed the same inspiring belief in his subordinates that Bennis' later mentor, Douglas McGregor, developed into 'Theory Y.'

Over the years Bennis has modified his thinking several times on whether leadership can be taught, or only learned experientially. 'I don't yet know enough about human thinking to be sure that leadership can or cannot be taught,' he said in 1997. But after teaching an undergraduate class at USC for two years he tends to think that ideas do have the power to change mindsets and behaviour.

To Bennis, the paramount factor in developing leaders is developing the self. In his workbook *Learning to Lead* (1997) he emphasizes the need for an 'integrated self' before leadership qualities can emerge.

Despite his famous aphorism about managers and leaders, he doesn't believe there is a complete dichotomy between them. 'Some have said you can't be both. I don't agree; there are examples of both in one person. I believe in "possible selves" – the capacity to adapt and change.'

Bennis regards himself as more of a journalist than a guru (in his seventies he is fulfilling a student ambition to be a playwright) and has an eye for the memorable quote. He is fond of quoting a little-known aphorism by Winston Churchill: 'The emperor of the future will be the emperor of ideas.'

Warren Bennis sees the leader, the person who transforms an organization, as 'the social architect' – a concept anticipated before World War II by Chester Barnard. Tom Peters has acknowledged that, 25 years before *In Search of Excellence*, Bennis had perceived much of what Peters and Waterman identified as landmarks of the excellent company.

In *The Unconscious Conspiracy – Why Leaders Can't Lead*, Bennis pointed up the ability of leaders to bring about change by positive motivation: 'In a study of school teachers, it turned out that when they held high expectations of their students, that alone was enough to cause an increase of 25 points in the students' IQ scores.'

Leadership, says Bennis, is 'probably the most studied and

least understood of any management subject.' His favourite definition of the attribute is: 'The capacity to create a compelling vision and translate it into action and sustain it.' The best leaders, he says, are 'ideas people, conceptualists.' But he describes leadership as 'an endless subject and endlessly interesting because you can never get your conceptual arms fully around it. I always feel rather like a lepidopterist chasing a butterfly' (*Director* magazine, April, 1991).

The four key abilities identified in Bennis's 1985 study of 90 successful US public figures are: the management of attention, the management of meaning (communications), the management of trust and the management of self. The first he attributes to a vision that others can believe in and adopt as their own. Vision is about the long term; market imperatives are short term. 'With a vision,' says Bennis, 'the leader provides the all-important bridge from the present to the future of the organization.' Among examples he cites are Lee Iacocca at Chrysler, President John F. Kennedy and civil rights leader Martin Luther King. (Two of those three, of course, were assassinated; the great and permanent risk of strong political leadership.)

Communicating vision and translating it into successful results for the organization is the second of Bennis' required leadership skills; the management of meaning. This, he explains, is why Ronald Reagan was deemed a more successful president than the better-informed, more thoughtful Jimmy Carter.

The mission credo of Johnson & Johnson translates vision into practical daily guidelines. General Motors under chief executive Roger Smith placed a high value on getting the company's long-term vision shared by all employees.

Trust, the third key factor to leadership skills, is described by Bennis as 'the emotional glue that binds followers and leaders together.' He believes leaders have to be consistent, and in the late 1980s cited Margaret Thatcher as a prime example – 'focused, constant, and all of a piece.'

Self-management, the fourth quality, means persistence, self-knowledge, willingness to take risks, commitment and challenge. Above all, it means willingness to go on learning, and in particular to learn from adversity and failure. 'The learning person looks forward to failures or mistakes. The worst problem in leadership is basically early success.'

In *Leaders*, Bennis and Nanus concluded that the most impressive and memorable quality of the individuals they studied was 'the way they responded to failure . . . They simply don't think about failure, don't even use the word, relying on such synonyms as "mistake", "glitch", "bungle", or countless others.'

On Becoming a Leader (1989) and *Learning to Lead* (1997) both address how leadership can be developed in the field. The first tackles three practical questions: how people learn to lead, how an organization can encourage or unwittingly stifle leadership qualities, and how leadership can be taught. His case studies are of less familiar personalities than those in *Leaders: Strategies for Taking Charge*, consisting of 29 American personalities from feminists to film-makers. *Learning to Lead* is a practical workbook, previously available only on the US college circuit, which addresses itself primarily to developing personal character and qualities as a basis for leadership.

Organizing Genius, Bennis' 1997 study of how dynamic project groups are formed and led, written with Patricia Ward Biederman, is in many ways his most interesting book, the fruit of 40 years' fascination with the workings of 'creative collaboration' under the pressure of make-or-break deadlines and intense competition. The projects studied range from the race against Nazi Germany to perfect the first atomic weapon and Lockheed's development of advanced military aircraft such as the U2 spy plane and the Stealth bomber through Walt Disney's brilliant animated films to the Xerox and Apple teams that developed the first personal computers.

Although the book skirts around the central question of how organizations can sustain the dedicated creativity of such groups once projects come to an end, it is highly relevant to knowledge industries and to the coming era when, Bennis believes, team leadership rather than the charismatic individual leader will be the model for global businesses. In the 1980s, *On Becoming a Leader* bestowed almost iconic status on the individual achiever, but by 1997 Bennis had come to think that the heroic 'great man' model was not going to work in the very different organizations of the 1990s and the 21st century, except in circumstances where one inspirational person was needed to change an entire culture.

On a personal note, he told *Director* magazine in 1991 that true leaders needed the humility to learn from the people they led. 'My heroes are the people who are continuous learners, who have their eyebrows always raised in curiosity and who can say to themselves: "The more vulnerable I am to my people, the more I can influence them".'

While Bennis remains the acknowledged world guru on leadership theory, contenders are staking out their own areas of the field, such as Harvard's John P. Kotter (qv), who concentrates principally on the leadership of organizations and leader/manager differentials, and a European authority, Dutch-born Manfred Kets de Vries of INSEAD, the international business school near Paris, who writes from a psychological perspective. In Britain, John Adair developed an approach learned from his experience as a lecturer at Sandhurst military academy and now holds Europe's only chair of leadership, at Exeter University.

KEY WRITINGS

Bennis, W. (1968) *The Temporary Society*, New York: Harper and Row.

Bennis, W. (1976) *The Unconscious Conspiracy*, New York: Amacon Press.

Bennis, W. and Nanus, B. (1985) *Leaders: the Strategies for Taking Charge*, New York: Harper and Row.

Bennis, W. (1989) *On Becoming a Leader*, London: Business Books.

Bennis, W. (1993) *An Invented Life: Reflections on Leadership and Change*, New York: Addison-Wesley.

Bennis, W. and Townsend, R. (1995) *Reinventing Leadership: Strategies to Empower the Organization*, London: Piatkus.

Bennis, W. and Biederman, P. (1997) *Organizing Genius*, New York: Addison-Wesley, Longman Inc.; London: Nicholas Brealey.
Bennis, W. and Goldsmith, J. (1997) *Learning to Lead*, New York: Addison-Wesley, Longman Inc.; London: Nicholas Brealey.

EDWARD DE BONO

(b. 1933)

Lateral thinking: 'the generation of new ideas and the escape from old ones'

Malta-born, Oxford-educated psychology and medical graduate who invented the concept of lateral thinking, now entered in the *Oxford English Dictionary* as 'seeking to solve problems by unorthodox or apparently illogical methods.'

De Bono is the foremost example of a guru who has built a reputation out of one 'Big Idea'. Describing himself as 'a thinker about thinking,' he has generated nearly 50 books out of his brainwave, along with a highly lucrative career in teaching, lecturing and consultancy.

His central argument, derived from his medical experience, is that humans are quite good at processing with mathematics, statistics and computers, but have done very little about perception and creativity (functions that computers are unable to carry out). It was also from medicine that he derived his ideas of the patterning behaviour of self-organizing systems. His book *The Mechanism of Mind*, published in 1969, was about 20 years ahead of its time.

Among the world-class companies to whom he has acted as consultant are Shell, IBM, Exxon, 3M, Apple, Id, Citibank, General Foods, Procter & Gamble and Unilever. His International Creative Forum brings together leading corporations in different fields to focus on the introduction of 'serious creativity' into their organizations. He has also been retained by governments and non-business organizations such as police forces and he runs the world's largest curriculum programme for the direct teaching of thinking in schools.

De Bono has taught at Oxford, Cambridge, London and Harvard universities and is the founder-director (since 1971) of the Cognitive Research Trust in Cambridge and the Centre for the Study of Thinking. He now spends much of his time working for the Supranational Independent Thinking Organization in The Hague.

His books have been translated into 25 languages and his work is academically respected in countries as different as Venezuela and the Soviet Union.

'The purpose of lateral thinking,' says Edward de Bono in *Lateral Thinking for Management* (1971) 'is the generation of new ideas and the escape from old ones.' He likens the process to developing a cross-reference technique for a filing system set up to store data in a particular way. Creativity, he says, 'involves breaking out of established patterns in order to look at things in a different way,' and creativity, he points out, comes into every aspect of managing a business – not only innovation but information systems, communications, finance, marketing, advertising and promotion, labour relations, problem solving, planning, design, R&D and public relations.

De Bono differentiates lateral thinking from 'vertical' or traditional, logical thinking, which proceeds step by step 'directly from one state of information to another state . . . One of the characteristic features of vertical thinking is continuity. One of the characteristic features of lateral thinking is discontinuity.'

The two systems do not cancel each other out, but are complementary. Where vertical thinking operates on a 'Yes/No' progression of alternatives, seeking always the solution that is right, lateral thinking proceeds by provocative leaps in unlikely directions, seeking what can be used in an idea rather than accepting or rejecting the whole idea outright. Quite often both systems come up with the same solution, says de Bono, but one can increase the chances of success by developing skills in lateral thinking.

In practice, he suggests, one could use lateral thinking for five per cent of the time and vertical thinking for the other 95 per cent, operating the systems alternately: 'lateral thinking turns up an idea, vertical thinking develops it.' Vertical thinking comes into its own in testing the creative ideas turned up by lateral thinking, and for transforming them into a plan of action. Lateral thinking, says its inventor, is not a method for decision-making.

De Bono's books on lateral thinking offer a system for teaching oneself the skill. High among his training 'tools' is the 'operational', nonsense-word PO, which acts like a railway signal to switch thinking patterns onto new tracks. In one of de Bono's examples, considering the problem of how to reduce traffic congestion in cities, use of PO triggers the 'intermediate impossible' solution of square wheels for cars. The underlying truth of that is how to make driving difficult or unpleasant and thereby discourage use of cars: more practical solutions could be a tax on road use or physical ridges in the road.

Other 'discontinuity' techniques include the use of analogy and 'random word' association to break the chain of vertical thinking. *Lateral Thinking for Management* also provides guidelines for formal brainstorming sessions and group practices for executives. De Bono summarizes the lateral thinking process in five steps:

• Escape from clichés and fixed patterns
• Challenge assumptions
• Generate alternatives
• Jump to new ideas and then see what happens
• Find new entry points from which to move forward

In applying its uses to management, de Bono also looks to a future when the 'concept manager' will have an established role in a corporation, managing the 'concept capital' of the organization − creativity, new ideas, adapting to change, defining objectives. Until that time arrives, he suggests, the organization of lateral thinking as a management tool may fall to the training officer, the OR department, the planning department or R&D. It should not, he stresses, be the special preserve of any one department.

De Bono himself considers his most significant book to be *I Am Right, You Are Wrong* (Viking/Penguin 1990), which he claims challenges the whole basis of the West's thinking culture. It explains the difference between 'rock' and 'water' logic, why rock logic has restricted the full potential of thinking, and how water logic arises from a fuller understanding of how the brain works.

The oddly titled *Six Thinking Hats* (1985) provides a system for escaping from traditional argument and confrontational thinking to better exploration of a subject and a more creative outcome. It has been adopted by major corporations such as IBM, Prudential and Du Pont. De Bono is extending this system (in which imaginary 'hats' in different colours are donned to encourage specific mental functions: e.g. white for information, red for feeling and intuition, black for caution, yellow for benefits, green for creative thinking, blue for the organization of thinking) with a sequel called *Six Action Shoes*, which separates routine from emergency action.

De Bono believes that the usual approach to fostering creativity – relying on inspiration and release from inhibitions – is far too weak, and that the brain, not being naturally creative, requires the exercise of deliberate techniques to stimulate it. Although inevitably overlapping to some extent, his books and courses on thinking represent a genre he has made his own. A basic de Bono library is listed here.

KEY WRITINGS

De Bono, E. (1967) *The Use of Lateral Thinking*, Maidenhead: McGraw-Hill; London: Penguin.
De Bono, E. (1968) *The Five-Day Course in Thinking*,

Maidenhead: McGraw-Hill; London: Penguin.

De Bono, E. (1969) *The Mechanism of Mind*, Maidenhead: McGraw-Hill; London: Penguin.

De Bono, E. (1971) *Lateral Thinking for Management*, Maidenhead: McGraw-Hill; London: Penguin.

De Bono, E. (1982) *De Bono's Course in Thinking*, Maidenhead: McGraw-Hill; London: Penguin.

De Bono, E. (1985) *Conflicts: A Better Way to Resolve Them*, Maidenhead: McGraw-Hill; London: Penguin.

De Bono, E. (1985) *Tactics: The Art and Science of Success*, Maidenhead: McGraw-Hill; London: Penguin.

De Bono, E. (1985) *Six Thinking Hats*, London: Penguin.

De Bono, E. (1990) *I Am Right, You Are Wrong*, London: Viking.

De Bono, E. (1991) *Handbook for a Positive Revolution*, London: Penguin.

De Bono, E. (1991) *Practical Thinking*, London: Penguin.

De Bono, E. (1993) *Water Logic*, London: Penguin.

De Bono, E. (1994) *Parallel Thinking*, London: Penguin.

De Bono, E. (1995) *Teach Yourself to Think*, London: Penguin.

De Bono, E. (1996) *The Edward de Bono Book of Wisdom*, London: Penguin.

ALFRED D. CHANDLER

(b. 1918)

Structure follows strategy in organizations

US economic historian, Straus Professor of Business History at Harvard University since 1971, whose work on organizations has been largely based on studies of major US companies between 1850 and 1920; the period, as he sees it, when modern capitalism was shaped and a new economic unit came into being. This was the business with a range of distinct operating units, each managed autonomously and completely different from its historical predecessor, the traditional single-unit firm, personally owned and managed.

Chandler believes that his work contributed to a nationwide restructuring of corporations, with the multi-divisional form of organization becoming the standard for large industrial firms producing multiple products in multiple markets. He was one of the first management theorists to perceive the importance of creating a strategic plan for a business before framing its organizational structure.

His most influential book, *Strategy and Structure*, was used by AT&T executives in their restructuring exercise after the 1984 breakup of the telecommunications giant, and Chandler's theories were credited with helping to speed up the change of focus within AT&T from a service utility to an actively marketed sales organization.

Chandler's main contribution to management theory has been to explain the relationship in organizations between strategy and structure, from which he took the title of his best-known book, published in 1962. In *Strategy and Structure*, he demonstrates how the two are indissolubly linked in an organization, defining 'strategy' as the determination of long-term goals and objectives, courses of action and allocation of resources, and 'structure' as the way the organization is put together to administer the strategy, with all the hierarchies and lines of authority which that implies. Chandler is clear in his belief that structure follows strategy.

Like Weber, he believes that the managerial hierarchy system offers the best hope for long-term business prosperity, and he concentrates on the principle that the salaried manager's role is critical. 'The visible hand' of management, he observes in *Managerial Hierarchies*, replaced Adam Smith's 'invisible hand' of market forces by coordinating the flow of goods from producers to customers more efficiently and profitably than was achieved by simple market mechanisms. As managers receive power and authority through their official roles, so their careers become increasingly technical and professional.

Chandler was the first management writer to recognize the importance of the decentralization principle in a large corporation, which became the central tenet of so much business practice in the 1960s and 1970s. It had already contributed substantially to Alfred P. Sloan's restructuring of General Motors in the interwar years, but Sloan did not publish his own book until 1963.

Chandler was also an early advocate of the need to co-ordinate strategic planning from the centre to ensure longterm growth for the company, while allowing the individual units and their managers to get on with day-to-day tactics.

His guiding rule has always been that outside pressures dictate how firms evolve from Weber-style traditional, family-based businesses into large, hierarchical organizations – pressures born of the huge market expansions and technological changes of the late nineteenth and early twentieth centuries. He traces the first managerial hierarchies to the rapid expansion of US railroads in the 1850s and 1860s, when a need emerged for centralized scheduling but local management of a variety of functions in geographic divisions that were responsible for up to 100 miles of track.

In his studies of four great US corporations – General Motors, Sears Roebuck, Du Pont and Standard Oil – Chandler looks at how these companies responded to similar external pressures either by positive strategies such as seeking new markets or diversifying products, or by negative, defensive strategies such as vertical integration with suppliers to protect a market position.

Some were more successful than others: Standard Oil, in Chandler's view, was slow to respond with a decentralized structure in the 1920s because of a failure to understand how structure should follow strategy.

Chandler's analysis of corporate development in the different markets and economies of Europe as well as in the US have led him to conclude that 'only by comparing the evolution of large-scale multi-unit enterprises in different economies can organizational imperatives be identified and the impact of the cultural attitudes and values, ideologies, political systems, and social structures that affect these imperatives be understood.'*

In each case, however, the structure of a management hierarchy followed the creation of the multi-unit business and enabled it to function through delegation of responsibility.

*From *Managerial Hierarchies: Comparative Perspectives on the Rise of Modern Industrial Enterprises*, ed. by A. D. Chandler and H. Deams (Harvard University Press, 1980), quoted in *Organizational Theory*, ed. D. S. Pugh (Penguin, 1990)

KEY WRITINGS

Chandler, A. D. (1962) *Strategy and Structure*, Massachusetts: MIT Press.

Chandler, A. D. (1977) *The Visible Hand: The Managerial Revolution in American Business*, Cambridge, Mass.: Harvard University Press.

Chandler, A. D. and Deams, H. (eds) (1980) *Managerial Hierarchies: Comparative Perspectives on the Rise of Modern Industrial Enterprises*, Cambridge, Mass.: Harvard University Press.

Chandler, A. D. and Tedlow, R. S. (1985) *The Coming of Managerial Capitalism*, Toronto: Irwin.

W. EDWARDS DEMING

(1900–1993)

The key to quality: reducing variation

US statistician and founding father of the quality movement, who was responsible, with his fellow-American
Joseph Juran, for instilling the quality philosophy into
postwar Japanese industry. The message had been
rejected or ignored by American companies and was only
re-imported after Japanese manufacturing began its competitive march into American markets.

Deming and Juran remain icons of Japanese industry,
whose companies compete annually for a Deming Prize,
awarded since 1951 for major improvements in quality.
Both men were honoured by the Emperor with the Order
of the Sacred Treasure, second class, the highest Japanese
award ever given to foreigners.

Deming is regarded by the Japanese as the chief architect of their phenomenal industrial success, but his home
country only began to recognize him in 1980, as a result
of an NBC television documentary on Japanese industry
called 'If Japan Can, Why Can't We?' Overnight,
American industry discovered his existence. Now he is
revered internationally for his simple yet revolutionary
principle that all processes are vulnerable to loss of
quality through variation: if the levels of variation are
managed, they can be decreased and quality raised.
Deming conducted seminars across the US until well into
his nineties. A frugal man, he had no formal organization

or consultancy but worked from a basement office in his Washington home.

After US industry finally woke up to Deming's theories, several large corporations suffering intractable problems came to credit Deming as the key to their revival; most notably Ford Motor Company in the early 1970s. Nashua Corporation in New Hampshire, a Fortune 500 company making computer disks, copiers and other office products, was one of the first Western companies to adopt Deming's principles. Nashua subsequently managed to cut its order-entry lead times from eight days to one hour and achieved a 70 per cent reduction in customer claims.

William E. Conway, Nashua's president and later chief executive officer, who 'discovered' Deming when the guru was 78, has called him 'the father of the Third Wave of the Industrial Revolution' for the way in which he developed statistical control of quality levels into a new way of managing business. 'The Japanese manufacturers utilizing the statistical control of quality are sweeping the world in the second half of the 20th century, just as American manufacturers utilizing mass production swept the world in the first half,' said Conway.

In the UK, Sir John Egan applied Deming principles to turning round the ailing fortunes of Jaguar Cars in the early 1980s. Egan wrote of Deming's 1986 book *Out of the Crisis* that it was 'required reading for every chief executive in British industry who is serious about ensuring the international competitiveness of his company' (*Director* Magazine, September 1988).

Deming, an electrical engineer by training (University of Wyoming, 1921) and a Ph.D. in mathematical physics from Yale, worked for a time in the 1920s at the Western Electric Hawthorne plant in Chicago where Elton Mayo carried out his famous experiments in communication and motivation. Here Deming discovered the work of Walter Shewhart, the pioneer of controlled and uncontrolled variables and the statistical control of processes. He later became a statistician for the US government, working on data for the national census of 1939/40. In 1942 he set up courses to teach Shewhart's methods to industrialists and engineers. After the war he was invited to Japan by General MacArthur to advise on the Japanese census. Contacts made then resulted in the watershed invitation of 1950 which was to have such reverberating effects.

Deming's approach to quality control is basically that of a statistician (his compatriot and fellow quality guru J. M. Juran has criticized him for it), but it is also firmly rooted in the belief that quality is about people, not products – an approach which made a particular impact on the Japanese. He also believed that 85 per cent of production faults are the responsibility of management, not workers. The famous Deming 'Fourteen Points' of management are at the heart of his philosophy.

In 1950, when W. Edwards Deming made his first visit to Japan, the country was still recovering from the atomic bombing raids of August 1945. The economy was struggling to stand upright, much less move ahead, and Japanese goods still suffered from their prewar reputation for shoddiness.

Deming embarked on an exhausting series of lectures to engineers, from 8am to 5pm day after day in punishing heat. 'I was dripping wet by 8.30am,' he recalled in the BBC2 television series *Nippon*. 'The Japanese appreciated it. They were sorely afraid that they had established a reputation for shoddy quality and that they could never undo it. I assured them that it would take only a short while to undo that reputation and develop a new one.

'I think I was the only man in Japan in 1950 who believed my prediction – that within five years manufacturers the world over would be screaming for protection. It took four years.'

The core element in this apparent miracle was the 'management circle' – still known in Japan as the 'Deming circle' – of planning, implementation, check and action. Above all, it rested on the belief in 'Management for Quality' (Deming uses this term where Juran 'brands' his approach as 'Company-Wide Quality').

Deming's basic management philosophy, as impressed on his eager Japanese audiences, was to regard the consumer as 'the most important part of the production line.' Developing this in *Out of the Crisis* (1984), he insisted that merely having a satisfied customer was not enough. 'Profit in business comes from repeat customers, customers that boast about your product and service, and that bring friends with them.'

Deming always taught the necessity of staying ahead of the customer, anticipating what his needs will be in years to come.

His Fourteen Points for management were developed over some twenty years and were still being refined and re-worded by the master in the 1990s. Henry Neave, author of *The Deming Dimension* (SPC Press, Knoxville, 1990), explains that they are not instructions or techniques, but rather 'vehicles for opening up the mind to new thinking, to the possibility that there are radically different and better ways of organizing our businesses and working with people.'

These, as quoted in Neave's book and Deming's own words, are the basic Fourteen Points:

1. Create constancy of purpose for continual improvement of products and service.
2. Adopt the new philosophy created in Japan.
3. Cease dependence on mass inspection: build quality into the product in the first place.
4. End lowest-tender contracts; instead, require meaningful measures of quality along with price.
5. Improve constantly and forever every process for planning, production and service.
6. Institute modern methods of training on the job for all, including management.
7. Adopt and institute leadership aimed at helping people to do a better job.
8. Drive out fear, encourage effective two-way communication.

9. Break down barriers between departments and staff areas.
10. Eliminate exhortations for the workforce – they only create adversarial relationships.
11. Eliminate quotas and numerical targets. Substitute aid and helpful leadership.
12. Remove barriers to pride of workmanship, including annual appraisals and Management By Objectives.
13. Encourage education and self-improvement for everyone.
14. Define top management's permanent commitment to ever-improving quality and productivity, and their obligation to implement all these principles.

The Fourteen Points are comprehensively expounded, chapter by chapter, in *The Deming Dimension*, a fascinating exposition of the guru's work and its development since publication of *Out of the Crisis*.

Deming himself said: 'If I had to reduce my message for management to just a few words, I'd say it all had to do with reducing variation.'

KEY WRITINGS

Deming, W. E. (1982) *Quality, Productivity and Competitive Position*, Massachusetts: MIT, Center for Advanced Engineering Study.
Deming, W. E. (1986, 1988) *Out of the Crisis*, Massachusetts: MIT, Center for Advanced Engineering Study; Cambridge: Cambridge University Press.
Walton, Mary (1986,1989) T*he Deming Management Method*, New York: Dodd, Mead and Co.; London: Mercury Books.
Neave, H. R. (1990) *The Deming Dimension*, Knoxville, Tennessee: SPC Press; available in the UK through the British Deming Association, 2 Castle Street, Salisbury, Wilts SP1 1BB.

10

PETER DRUCKER

(b. 1909)

Primary tasks for effective managers

The management guru's management guru. Born in Vienna during the heyday of that city's pre-1914 culture, Drucker has invented or prefigured most of the leading management theories of the last half-century, from 'Management by Objectives' to privatization; from putting the customer first to the role of the chief executive in corporate strategy; from 'structure follows strategy' to 'stick to the knitting'; from decentralization to the implications of the information age and the rise of the 'knowledge worker,' a term he coined in 1969.

His five basic principles of management remain as valid as ever: setting objectives, organizing, motivating and communicating, establishing measurements of performance and developing people.

Tom Peters, whose co-authored book *In Search of Excellence* developed many Drucker ideas, says the Viennese sage deserves much of the credit for 'moving 75 to 80 per cent of the Fortune 500 to radical decentralization,' adding that no true 'discipline of management' existed before Drucker.

For many years a pillar of New York University Business School, Drucker since 1971 has been Clarke Professor of Social Science at Claremont Graduate School, Claremont, California. He is still writing prolifically in his eighties, adding to the 24-odd books he has published since *The End of Economic Man* appeared in 1939. They divide almost equally between works on management theory and technique and works of economic, political and social analysis. Many of the latter are seminal works which mapped out whole landscapes of the future with much wider horizons than those bounded by management. Philip Sadler, vice-president and former director of Ashridge Management College, found his thinking entirely changed by Drucker's 1969 book *The Age of Discontinuity*, which for Sadler pointed clearly to the coming decline of Britain's manufacturing industry.

This book, still well worth study, prefigured many of the business best-sellers of the late 1980s and early 1990s on managing chaos and disruptive change. Drucker's books have anticipated those of Charles Handy (qv), Tom Peters (qv) and Richard Pascale (qv) – to name only three. In some of its ideas, *The Age of Discontinuity* was 20 years ahead of John Naisbitt's *Megatrends* and Charles Handy's *The Age of Unreason*.

It was in *The Age of Discontinuity*, incidentally, that Drucker introduced the concept of privatization, though he called it 'reprivatization.' He accurately forecast the disillusionment with government arising from the discovery that governments could not, after all, produce miracles. 'There is little doubt, for instance, that the British in adopting the National Health Service believed that medical care would cost nothing . . . . Nurses, doctors, hospitals, drugs and so on have to be paid for by somebody. But everybody expected this "somebody" to be somebody else.'

Drucker advocated privatization on the grounds that the purpose of government was to govern, not to 'do', and that the two roles were incompatible. His vision, unlike the Conservative Party's realization of it, was for privatization to cover all institutions, not merely business ones – universities, for example.

A year or so after publication of *The Age of Discontinuity*, the word privatization made its first appearance in a Conservative Central Office pamphlet, in May 1970 ('A New Style of Government'), crediting Drucker with the coinage.

The son of an Austrian government official who helped found the Salzburg Festival, Drucker came to Britain in the late 1920s, and his first job was as an apprentice clerk in a Bradford wool exporting firm, working with a quill pen in 80-pound brassbound ledgers chained to the desk. Between 1933 and 1936 he worked as an economist in a London merchant bank and then decided to throw in his lot with the United States. He emigrated to the US in 1937, produced his first book two years later and in 1942 took a consultant's job with General Motors, then the world's largest company.

Out of this experience came his influential 1946 book *Concept of the Corporation*, still one of the best and most perceptive analyses of the successful large organization. As well as General Motors, other companies studied in the book were General Electric, IBM and Sears Roebuck, and Drucker identified their success with certain managerial characteristics, notably delegation and goal-setting (Management By Objectives) and certain structural characteristics, such as decentralization.

Drucker believed that the ultimate key to success in all these companies was that 'they knew what businesses they were in, what their competencies were and how to keep their efforts focused on their goals' (*Organization Theory*, ed. D. S. Pugh). Nearly 30 years later Peters and Waterman reached much the same conclusion, set out in more populist style, in their best-seller *In Search of Excellence*.

Concept of the Corporation also analysed the importance of marketing – at that time an almost universally neglected function – and the delicate balance which a company must seek to achieve between long-term strategy and short-term performance.

Drucker figures in more management-book indexes than any other individual by far. In *Makers of Management*, by David Clutterbuck and Stuart Crainer, he rates no fewer than 40 separate page references.

Peter Drucker's reputation as a management guru was established with *The Practice of Management* (1954), a work still regarded by later theorists as one of the best and clearest in the field. In this, he identified Management By

Objectives as the first of seven primary tasks of management. MBO, dignified with capital letters, became a movement of its own, and Britain's John Humble (qv) made a speciality of developing its theory and practice.

Management by objectives emerged out of Drucker's work with General Electric among his studies for *Concept of the Corporation*. Each GE manager was responsible for a profit centre and given targets to achieve – seven per cent return on sales and 20 per cent return on investment. These were severely applied; you lost your job if you didn't meet them.

Drucker perceived that, since businesses survive or fall by the bottom line, corporate goals should be divided into objectives and clearly assigned to units and individuals. 'Management by objectives,' as Richard Pascale observes in *Managing on the Edge*, 'ensures that each link in the chain of command does its part . . .'

A subsequent handbook, *Managing for Results* (1964) is, in Drucker's own words of introduction, a 'what to do book.' It was, he believed, 'the first attempt at an organized presentation of the economic tasks of the business executive and the first halting step towards a discipline of economic performance in business enterprise.' It sets out in clear, nononsense prose, guidelines for understanding business realities and for analysing a company in terms of revenues, resources, prospects, cost centres, customer needs, building on strengths, finding potential, making key decisions and building strategies for the future. It is still one of the best practical vade-mecums for anyone running a business enterprise. Drucker believes that every three years or so a company should be put under the microscope and every product, process, technology, service or market subjected to a gruelling assessment.

Throughout his work, Drucker's emphasis has been on the effectiveness of managers – particularly in making good use of their human resources – as the key to a productive and profitable organization. Management, says Drucker, is the job of organizing resources to achieve the satisfactory performance of an enterprise. Managers must in the end be measured by their economic performance, though this is not necessarily synonymous with maximum profits; rather, with sufficient profit that will cover the risks which have been taken, and to avoid the enterprise making a loss. Management by objectives is the key to this.

Drucker has sometimes been criticized for neglecting theories of motivation, though he was one of the first to recognize and praise Douglas McGregor's Theory Y of consultative management as early as 1954.

Drucker's emphasis on objective-setting for management is most clearly set out in his mammoth compendium *Management: Tasks, Responsibilities, Practices* (1973). This represents an encyclopedia of his earlier writings and is recommended as the bedrock of any aspiring manager's reading list. Studded with illuminating case studies, the massive volume (weighing 3½ pounds in hardback) defines every aspect of managerial skills and pinpoints eight areas where clear objectives are vital: marketing, innovation, human organization, financial resources, physical resources, productivity, social responsibility and profit requirements. A thorough grounding in this vast work is virtually the equivalent of a do-it-yourself business-school course.

Shortly before this was published, Drucker had defined his broad view of management in *People and Performance* (1973): 'To fulfil the specific purpose and mission of the organization; to make work productive and the worker achieving; and to manage social impacts and social responsibility.'

In *Management: Tasks, Responsibilities, Practices*, he identified five basic operations in the work of the manager, which together 'result in the integration of resources into a viable growing organism.' These summarize the essentials of management with more clarity than any other book before or since:

A manager, in the first place, sets objectives. He determines what the objectives should be. He determines what the goals in each area of objectives should be. He decides what has to be done to reach these objectives. He makes the objectives effective by communicating them to the people whose performance is needed to attain them.

Second, a manager organizes. He analyses the activities, decisions and relations needed. He classifies the work. He divides it into manageable activities and further divides the activities into manageable jobs. He groups these units and jobs into an organization structure. He selects people for the management of these units and for the jobs to be done.

Next, a manager motivates and communicates. He makes a team out of the people that are responsible for various jobs. He does that through the practices with which he works. He does it in his own relations to the men with whom he works. He does it through his 'people decisions' on pay, placement and promotion. And he does it through constant communication, to and from his subordinates, and to and from his superior, and to and from his colleagues.

The fourth basic element in the work of the manager is measurement. The manager establishes yardsticks – and few factors are as important to the performance of the organization and of every man in it. He sees to it that each man has measurements available to him which are focused on the performance of the whole organization and which, at the same time, focus on the work of the individual and help him do it. He analyses, appraises and interprets performance. As in all other areas of his work, he communicates the meaning of the measurements and their findings to his subordinates, to his superiors, and to colleagues.

Finally, a manager develops people, including himself.

Taking an historical perspective, Drucker has since identified seven key elements in postwar management development:

1. Scientific management of work as the key to productivity
2. Decentralization as a basic principle of organization
3. Personnel management as the orderly way of fitting people into organization structures
4. Manager development to provide for the needs of tomorrow

5. Managerial accounting – use of analysis and information as the foundation for firm decision-making
6. Marketing
7. Long-range planning

In recent years, Drucker's books have included *Innovation and Entrepreneurship* (1985), a typically wide-ranging study of growth sectors of the US economy in the early 1980s, including many businesses not normally considered as such: private health care, for example, non-profit-making private schools and public/private partnerships in which government units contract out services to competitive private companies. *The New Realities* (1989) ranged over a global stage, anticipating the development of such contemporary phenomena as the transnational economy, the democratization of the Soviet republics, the changing ethos of the United States and the demands of a post-industrial, post-business society. *Post-Capitalist Society* (1992) examined among other phenomena the division of society into knowledge and service workers, and the economic and social challenges involved.

Drucker's breadth of vision and eclectic range of publications spring from his belief that management is central to life, not merely to business. One of his recurring concepts is that of the chief executive as conductor of an orchestra. As he says: 'We are beginning to realise that management itself is the central institution of our present society, and that there are very few differences between managing a business, managing a diocese, managing a hospital, managing a university, managing a research lab, managing a labour union or managing a government agency. All along, this has been the main thrust of my work, and the one that distinguishes it from practically all my contemporaries working in the field.'

Rosabeth Moss Kanter (qv) views his goals as even more embracing. In an article in *New Management* (winter 1985), she wrote: 'Good management is also our best hope for world peace. In the Drucker perspective, imperatives for growth push organizations beyond national borders in the search for new markets. The world becomes inter-connected by a series of cross-cutting trade relationships in which the interests of managers in the survival of their multinational enterprises outweigh the interests of politicians. Quality of life, technological progress and world peace, then, are all the products of good management . . . At root, Drucker is a management utopian, descended as much from Robert Owen as Max Weber.'

To Drucker, the business organization, as any organization, is 'a human, a social, indeed a moral phenomenon.' Customer service rather than profit should dominate management thinking, profit being the means of continued investment in innovation and improvement.

'Contrary to the approach to the study of political and social organization that has prevailed in the West since Machiavelli, I stressed all along that organization does not deal with power but with responsibility. This is the keynote of my work that has remained constant over more than 40 years.'

Drucker sums up his own vast contribution to management thinking in these words, quoted in *Makers of Management* (Clutterbuck and Crainer):

'I was the first one to see that the purpose of a business lies outside of itself – that is, in creating and satisfying a customer. I was the first to see the decision process as central, the first to see that structure has to follow strategy, and the first one to see, or at least the first to say, that management has to be management by objectives and self-control.'

KEY WRITINGS

Drucker, P. F. (1946) *Concept of the Corporation*, New York: John Day.

Drucker, P. F. (1951) *The New Society*, London: Heinemann.

Drucker, P. F. (1954) *The Practice of Management*, New York: Harper and Row.

Drucker, P. F. (1964, 1989) *Managing for Results*, London: Heinemann.

Drucker, P. F. (1969) *The Age of Discontinuity*, London: Heinemann.

Drucker, P. F. (1974) *Management: Tasks, Responsibilities, Practices*, London: Heinemann; New York: Harper and Row.

Drucker, P. F. (1985) *Innovation and Entrepreneurship*, London: Heinemann.

Drucker, P. F. (1989, 1990) *The New Realities*, London: Heinemann Professional Publishing; Mandarin Paperback.

Drucker, P. F. (1992) *Post-Capitalist Society*, Oxford: Butterworth Heinemann.

Drucker, P. F. (1994) *Frontiers of Management*, Oxford: Butterworth Heinemann.

Drucker, P. F. (1997) *Drucker on Asia*, Oxford: Butterworth Heinemann.

Drucker, P. F. (1998) *On the Profession of Management*, Boston: Harvard Business School Press.

11

HENRI FAYOL

(1841–1925)

Five foundation stones of modern management

French mining engineer and manager, generally regarded
as the first to ask 'what is management?', to analyse the
nature of managerial activity and to formulate a complete
theory of management, based on his own experience of
running the mining and metallurgical combine
Commentry-Fourchamboult-Decazeville.

Fayol was in his seventies before his ideas gained currency in print, and his classic work, *Administration
Industrielle et Générale*, was not published in English (as
General and Industrial Management) until 1949. His key
definitions of managerial activity – to plan, to organize,
to command, to coordinate and to control – remained
accepted wisdom until Henry Mintzberg's revealing
studies in the 1960s.

Henri Fayol was years ahead of his time in linking strategy
and organizational theory and in emphasizing the need for
management development and the qualities of leadership.
Igor Ansoff in *Corporate Strategy* (1965) said that Fayol
'anticipated imaginatively and soundly most of the more
recent analyses of modern business practice,' although Peter
Drucker in his great compendium *Management: Tasks,*

Responsibilities and Practice (1973), criticized the application of Fayol's functional approach to larger and more complex organizations than the one he knew and managed.

Fayol believed the same principles of management could be applied, regardless of size, to organizations of all kinds, whether industrial, commercial, governmental, political, or even religious. His five key elements of industrial management remain the foundation-stones on which all later gurus, to a greater or lesser extent, have built.

These five elements are: to forecast and plan; to organize; to command; to coordinate and to control. Fayol defined the first as 'examining the future and drawing up the plan of action'; the second as 'building up the structure, material and human, of the undertaking'; the third as 'maintaining activity among the personnel'; the fourth as 'binding together, unifying and harmonizing all activity and effort'; and the fifth as 'seeing that everything occurs in conformity with established rule and expressed command.'

An organization, therefore, begins with a strategic plan or definition of goals, progresses to a structure to put that plan into action, is carried forward by controlled activity between manager and workforce, has the work of its disparate departments harmonized by coordinated management and, finally, is subject to checks on the efficiency of its working, preferably by independent 'staff' departments separate from the functional departments.

Fayol believed that a manager obtained the best performance from his workforce by leadership qualities, by his knowledge of the business and his workers, and by the ability to instil a sense of mission. From his own long experience in industry, he distilled his 14 General Principles of Management:

1. Division of work with specialization allowing individuals to build up skills and become more productive. 'The object of division of work is to produce more and better work with the same effort.'
2. Authority, both official and personal, with matching responsibility. 'Generally speaking, responsibility is feared as much as authority is sought after, and fear of

responsibility paralyses much initiative and destroys many good qualities. A good leader should possess and infuse into those around him courage to accept responsibility.'

3. Discipline, 'in essence obedience, application, energy, behaviour and outward marks of respect observed in accordance with the standing agreements between the firm and its employees . . . When a defect in discipline is apparent or when relations between superiors and subordinates leave much to be desired . . . the ill mostly results from the ineptitude of the leaders.'

4. Unity of command: each man should have only one boss with no conflicting lines of command. 'In all human associations, in industry, commerce, army, home, State, dual command is a perpetual source of conflicts . . .'

5. Unity of direction: 'one head and one plan for a group of activities having the same objective. It is the condition essential to unity of action, coordination of strength and focusing of effort.'

6. Subordination of individual to general interest, reconciling conflicting interests where necessary: 'That represents one of the great difficulties of management.' Means of effecting it are (1) firmness and good example on the part of superiors (2) agreements as fair as possible (3) constant supervision.

7. Fair remuneration for effort. 'Every mode of payment likely to make the personnel more valuable and improve its lot in life, and also to inspire keenness on the part of employees at all levels, should be a matter for managers' constant attention.'

8. Centralization or decentralization, the choice to depend on the condition of the business and the culture of its staff. 'The finding of the measure which shall give the best overall yield; that is the problem of centralisation or decentralization. Everything which goes to increase the importance of the subordinate's role is decentralization, everything which goes to reduce it is centralization.'

9. The scalar chain or hierarchical principle of management; a path 'dictated both by the need for some

transmission and by the principle of unity of command, but it is not always the swiftest . . . It is an error to depart needlessly from the line of authority but an even greater one to keep to it when detriment to the business ensues . . . When an employee is obliged to choose between the two practices, and it is impossible for him to take advice from his superiors, he should be courageous enough and feel free enough to adopt the line dictated by the general interest.'

10. Order, both material and social: 'Social order demands precise knowledge of the human requirements and resources of the concern and a constant balance between these.'

11. Equity in the treatment of employees: 'the head of the business should strive to instil a sense of equity throughout all levels of the scalar chain.'

12. Stability of tenure among personnel: 'Generally the managerial personnel of prosperous concerns is stable, that of unsuccessful ones is unstable. Instability of tenure is at one and the same time cause and effect of bad running. Nevertheless, changes of personnel are inevitable . . . stability of tenure of personnel is also a question of proportion.'

13. Initiative: 'Thinking out a plan and ensuring its success is one of the keenest satisfactions for an intelligent man to experience. It is also one of the most powerful stimulants of human endeavour . . . The initiative of all, added to that of the manager and supplementing it if need be, represents a great source of strength for business . . . The manager must be able to sacrifice some personal vanity in order to grant this sort of satisfaction to subordinates.'

14. A sense of *esprit de corps*: essential for management to foster the morale of its workforce. 'Real talent is needed,' said Fayol, 'to coordinate effort, encourage keenness, use each person's abilities, and reward each one's merit without arousing possible jealousies and disturbing harmonious relations.'

KEY WRITINGS

Fayol, H., trans. Constance Storrs (1949) *General and Industrial Management*, London: Pitman.
Quotations taken from extract in *Organization Theory* (1990) ed. D. S. Pugh, London: Penguin Books.

GARY HAMEL

(b. 1955)

Core competencies and strategic intent

Fastest-rising star of the international guru circuit since 1994, when he published (with University of Michigan professor C.K. Prahalad) the much-acclaimed book *Competing for the Future*, which redefined and reignited interest in the uses of strategy. Essentially it shifted strategic thinking from positioning a company within its industry to changing the rules of that industry and creating new markets. As a result of the book and the lecture circuit fame that followed, core competencies, strategic intent and industry foresight are just a few of Hamel's trademark concepts that have passed into the language of management.

Hamel started his career as a hospital administrator and switched tracks in 1978 to take a PhD in international business at the University of Michigan, where he met Indian-born Prahalad, then a newly hired associate professor of strategy and now professor of business administration and professor of corporate strategy and international business at Michigan's graduate school of business administration.

The pair quickly sparked ideas off each other and discovered a common belief, as Hamel wrote in the preface to their book, that 'the ultimate test of business school research is its managerial significance.' They have published seven influential articles in *Harvard Business Review* as well as their ground-breaking book, which advised companies to 'shine their headlights' on potential markets and customers ten years ahead, and to identify their core competencies that would enable them to refocus and reinvent their business for the future.

After ten years teaching strategy at London Business School, Hamel returned in 1993 to base himself in California's Silicon Valley, which he describes as 'a very good vantage point to see the future coming.' Here he heads a consultancy called Strategos Inc. in Menlo Park, just outside San Francisco, which generates annual revenues of around $20m out of advising companies on the Hamel brand of strategy as revolution.

'The capacity for strategic innovation,' he says, 'will be the next competitive edge for companies around the world.'

He is still a visiting professor of strategic management at LBS but with his easy, entertaining style of presentation he now rivals Tom Peters as a sought-after conference and seminar speaker, and was reported by the *Financial Times* in 1997 to earn as much as $150,000 for two days' work. He spends much of the year on the road, typically delivering a major speech every week. For his latest book, *Alliance Advantage: The Art of Creating Value Through Partnering* (1998), he joined forces with the heavyweight French management thinker Yves Doz, a professor at INSEAD, France's international business school.

Business strategy and strategic planning is riding high on the management agenda again after years of being sidelined in favour of shorter-term measures for operational efficiency such as re-engineering and downsizing, designed to counter the pressures of global competition and economic recession. Today's strategic approach is, however, very different from the systemic matrix planning popularized in the 1980s by Boston Consulting Group with the future of businesses classified as cash cows, dogs, stars and question marks.

Foremost among the new strategists is Gary Hamel, whose co-authored bestseller *Competing for the Future* sounded a necessary warning bell in the mid-1990s against the reflexive cost-cutting that was damaging companies' long-term growth prospects in the name of next quarter's results.

The book, which in classic fashion developed out of a landmark article in *Harvard Business Review* (July/August 1994), carried two powerful messages: first, that the sustainable health of a business could not be achieved by simply applying an accountant's rule to costs and second, that managers needed to look much farther into the future of the business than they had been accustomed to do. Customers and markets could not be relied upon to stay the same year on year, providing incremental profits: managers should ask themselves what the business would look like in the medium to long-term future and who their customers would be.

Hamel and Prahalad urged managers to ask themselves two sets of questions about their business, under the headings 'Today' and 'In the Future':

- Which customers do you serve today/will you serve in the future?
- Through what channels do you reach customers today/will you reach customers in the future?
- Who are your competitors today/who will be your competitors in the future?
- What is the basis for your competitive advantage today/what will be the basis for your competitive advantage in the future?
- Where do your margins come from today/where will your margins come from in the future?
- What skills or capabilities make you unique today/what skills or capabilities will make you unique in the future?

'If senior executives don't have reasonably detailed answers to the "future" questions, and if the answers they have are not significantly different from the "today" answers, there is little chance that their companies will remain market leaders,' warned Hamel and Prahalad.

The strength of their arguments against short-term solutions such as downsizing and in favour of seeking new growth strategy became evident in the years immediately following publication of their book. Leading business figures such as Howard Davies, deputy governor of the Bank of England and former chief executive of the Confederation of British Industry (CBI), began quoting the two gurus' devastating phrase 'corporate anorexia' about companies that had slimmed down so drastically that they had no resources to respond when growth opportunities returned.

A senior manager at ICI responsible for Asia Pacific liaison went on record in 1996 as saying that his company had gone so far in cutting corporate functions that it could no longer give promising managers career moves across boundaries and equip them to develop new markets as fully as in the past (Kennedy, Carol: 'The Incredible Shrinking Company,' *Director*, April 1996). At the pit of its cost-cutting, ICI had just two executive board directors responsible for splitting global operations between them – one for the eastern hemisphere and one for the west. More recently, the mighty Boeing Corporation was knocked off balance by a surge in its order-book that it no longer had the resources to meet, thanks to downsizing: its share price plunged as a result.

Hamel has since delved deeper into the processes of making strategy, which he stresses is distinct from planning. 'Strategy is revolution, everything else is tactics,' he argues. In Hamel's three key concepts, companies should build their *core competencies* to create *strategic intent* for their future business by practising *industry foresight*.

He divides companies into three categories:

- **The rule makers**, i.e., those which built their industries, such as IBM, Coca Cola and Merrill Lynch
- **The rule takers**, i.e., those which followed in the rule makers' wake but never quite caught up, such as McDonnell Douglas (trailing Boeing) and Avis, chasing Hertz

- **The rule breakers**, which are rewriting industry rules to their own bold agenda. Prime examples are Dell Computer, The Body Shop, Southwest Airlines, Swatch, the Virgin Group and Direct Line, First Direct, and all the other telephone-based financial services

The key to being a successful rule breaker is a willingness to redefine products and services by following certain guidelines. 'Any company intent on creating industry revolution has four tasks,' writes Hamel in *Harvard Business Review* ('Strategy as Revolution,' July/August 1996). 'First, the company must identify the unshakeable beliefs that cut across the industry – the industry's conventions. Second, the company must search for discontinuities in technology, lifestyles, working habits or geopolitics that might create opportunities to rewrite the industry's rules. Third, the company must achieve a deep understanding of its core competencies. Fourth, the company must use all this knowledge to identify the revolutionary ideas, the unconventional strategic options, that could be put to work in its competitive domain.'

Elsewhere in the article, Hamel describes nine 'routes to industry revolution,' including:

- 'Radically improving the value equation' (for example, the Swedish IKEA furniture stores, or the US company Fidelity Investments, which lowered the entry level to foreign equity funds to allow customers of modest means a slice of the action)
- 'Striving for individuality' (Levi Strauss now offer 'personal pair' outlets with computer-measured jeans)
- 'Increasing accessibility' (for example, direct telephone banking)

Other management theorists, notably W.Chan Kim and Renée Mauborgne, two professors of strategic management at INSEAD, are working along similar lines of lateral or creative thinking to break through accepted rules in an industry and thereby enhance or enlarge their customer base. Kim and Mauborgne call their theory 'value innovation' because it creates an entirely new dimension of value for the customer and thereby cuts out the competition.

Hamel also argues strongly that strategy should involve creativity at all levels of the organization, not just in the executive offices. 'One thing is certain,' he says. 'If you don't let the revolutionaries challenge you from within, they will eventually challenge you from without in the marketplace. . . When was the last time a Generation-X employee in your company exchanged ideas with the executive committee?'

Hamel summed up his core thinking to the *Financial Times* in April 1997: 'The test for any company today is whether they can tell me the five fundamental ways they are going to change their industry in the next ten years. If they can't, someone else will.'

KEY WRITINGS

Hamel, G. and Prahalad, C. K. (1994) 'Competing for the Future', Cambridge, Mass.: *Harvard Business Review*, (July/Aug), reprint no. 94403.

Hamel, G. and Prahalad, C. K. (1994) *Competing for the Future*, Boston: Harvard Business School Press.

Hamel, G. (1996) 'Strategy as Revolution', Cambridge, Mass.: *Harvard Business Review*, (July/Aug), reprint no. 96405.

13

MICHAEL HAMMER

(b. 1948)

The radical redesign of business processes

Computer scientist and mathematician who caused a management revolution in the early 1990s with the 'big idea' of re-engineering – identifying the key work processes in every aspect of a company's operations, following them across departments, stripping them down to their components and maximizing their efficiency. Hammer liked to declare he was 'reversing the Industrial Revolution', which – as Adam Smith described the workings of a pin factory – broke down processes into dozens of individual tasks.

Enthusiastically embraced by companies on both sides of the Atlantic desperate to counter the effects of recession, re-engineering has proved only patchily successful (surveys in the mid-1990s suggested that around 70 per cent of re-engineering efforts failed for one reason or another) and was often used as a cloak for 'downsizing' with cost-cutting redundancies. Yet in 1995 US companies spent more on re-engineering consultancy than the whole country spent on importing coffee.

Hammer became a lecture-circuit celebrity on the back of his 1990 *Harvard Business Review* article, 'Re-engineering Work: Don't Automate, Obliterate,' which was followed up in 1993 by a hugely best-selling book, *Reengineering the Corporation*, written with James Champy, a founder of the consultancy CSC Index.

The book sold more than two million copies world-wide and within a year of its publication 69 per cent of US companies surveyed by CSC Index, and 75 per cent of European companies, had undertaken re-engineering projects. Another survey by Price Waterhouse found that 78 per cent of Fortune 500 companies and 68 per cent of UK companies had adopted the technique. Soon re-engineering had moved out of manufacturing into service industries such as banking and into the public sector.

The book defined re-engineering as 'the fundamental rethinking and radical redesign of business processes to achieve dramatic improvements in critical measures of performance such as cost, quality, service and speed.' Its concept of rethinking was to take a blank sheet of paper and design the company as from scratch rather than innovate from existing practices or, in Hammer's colourful phrase, 'pave over the cow paths.' It seemed the answer to every organizational inefficiency.

In practice, however, there were many problems. Although some stunning productivity gains could be cited, and cycle times were often dramatically slashed, re-engineering became too mechanistic in implementation and simply ignored the human dimension. Hammer's early seminars, characterized by an aggressive dynamism and a barking delivery, were notable for a lack of attention to people issues. The charts looked impressive, but what of the people whose jobs were re-engineered out, and the traumatic impact on those who survived?

In 1995 Champy recognized this missing dimension with a book of his own, *Reengineering Management*, which addressed the issues of managing such radical change along with the challenge of inspiring, motivating and rewarding people to cooperate actively with it. Champy has since left CSC Index for Perot Systems, an offshoot of the EDS computer services giant founded by Ross Perot.

Hammer set up his own consultancy in Boston and has been lauded by *Time* magazine as one of America's most influential individuals. He has written two more books expanding and refining re-engineering (a term he and

Champy claim to have trademarked in its non-hyphenated spelling). In *Beyond Reengineering* (1997), he took a larger, more humanistic view of the 'process-centred organization,' emphasizing the entrepreneurial character of the customer-focused business, the individual ownership of processes and the need for teamwork and for employees to feel fulfilled by more than their pay-cheque.

Although Hammer is careful to say he discovered rather than invented re-engineering, he is a good example of the one-big idea guru who built his fame the classic way; from academic backwater research to *Harvard Business Review* article to best-selling book to lucrative consultancy and lecture work. Whatever happens to the reputation of re-engineering as a management theory, Hammer's work will undoubtedly continue to have an influence on the way companies are organized in the 21st century.

Re-engineering was an idea waiting to be reborn, in many ways harking back to the work-study theories of F.W. Taylor's 'scientific management' at the turn of the century. It germinated in study groups at Massachusetts Institute of Technology in the early 1980s where technology-minded academics brainstormed on how computers would shape 'the corporation of the 1990s,' and in similar work at the technology-based consultancy CSC Index, also located in Cambridge, Massachusetts. Hammer was a mathematician who had become a professor of computer science at MIT, and James Champy, his eventual collaborator, was the founder of CSC Index, where the term re-engineering was coined.

Like scientific management, re-engineering was a reassuringly hard-nosed term, unlike 'transformation' and some other buzzwords into which consultancies around the world would later absorb its principles. Its core concept centred on the process flows that cut across the departmental functions of a business, from factory floor to invoicing, but its streamlining of those processes by eliminating the number of wasteful tasks or 'handoffs' was not far removed from Taylor's belief in a 'one best way' to perform every industrial function.

Re-engineering is often known as business process re-engineering, or BPR, though Hammer and Champy eschewed this label, claiming it was too narrow in application and that true re-engineering involved a total rethink of management strategy as well as operational processes. The idea hit its moment as companies in the US and Europe were struggling with the severe recession of the early 1990s and were forced to search for new ways to make their operations more efficient and cost-effective.

Unfortunately, many attempts to implement it went off at half-cock or concentrated on cutting jobs, leading to the concept becoming damningly associated with downsizing and 'corporate anorexia.' This was a term coined by Gary Hamel (qv) and C.K. Prahalad in *Competing for the Future* to describe companies that had cut beyond the fat into the muscle and were too emaciated to seize growth opportunities. Charles Handy (qv) was quoted in *Fortune* in October 1994 as saying: 'The trouble with re-engineering when it is done badly – which it mostly is – is that it leaves people shattered, even the people left behind.'

Champy would later claim that only one in ten companies got re-engineering right. Only one in ten chief financial officers of US corporations in a May 1995 magazine survey (quoted in *The Witch Doctors* by John Micklethwait and Adrian Wooldridge) cited quality and service improvement as a reason for re-engineering rather than cost-cutting – perhaps a significant coincidence.

Certainly re-engineering can claim some spectacular successes – Ford Motor's accounting, Hallmark Cards and Federal Express are three well-known examples, and there are less high-profile examples in Britain such as Pilkington Optronics, the former periscope maker Barr and Stroud. Rolls-Royce Motor Cars was saved from near-bankruptcy in 1991 by application of re-engineering principles as part of a 'transformation' aided by Gemini Consulting. In all cases, the initiative was driven by dynamic leadership and in many, notably Rolls-Royce and British Telecom, it was part of a profound culture change.

Hammer always insisted that leadership was crucial to the success of the technique, saying: 'reengineering only succeeds when driven from the top levels of an organization.' What has been less recognized until recently is the importance of leadership at many levels, of owning the change processes and of energizing the whole organizational culture through communication and participation.

From being regarded as a change machine in its own right, re-engineering is now more wisely seen as part of an holistic approach, with a recognition that the technique works better for some areas of the business than others, and with more attention paid to human motivation and to the intellectual capital held in the heads of individual employees. The most successful change managers now encourage employees to feel involved and committed in the goals of change; to think of themselves as mini-entrepreneurs with a key role in the ultimate aim of delighting the customer.

In many companies, such as the Munich-based Siemens Nixdorf Informationssyteme (SNI), key workers are effectively responsible for re-engineering their own processes, and their ideas are exchanged and shared on the corporate intranet. To be fair to Hammer's original book, the case studies in *Reengineering the Corporation* did emphasize the added value to both company and individual when employees enjoyed more decision-making over their process work, as with the clerks in Ford's accounts payable department and the credit-checkers at IBM. But the style of Hammer's public speaking and writing has changed dramatically from a seminar he gave in Boston in 1993 when he declaimed with relish that re-engineering was 'not only about cutting the fat from an organization but grinding it up and frying it out.' In the final chapter of *Beyond Reengineering*, he even admits that the process-centred organization could turn into a nightmare.

'It may foster a brutal form of social Darwinism and a perverse modern Calvinism. . . It may also become confusing and disorienting to work and live in a process-centred world . . . Will we face spiritual poverty even as we enjoy material plenty? Will never-ending organizational improvement inevitably produce a culture of tension and stress? Will it destroy our very humanity?' Questions that might have come from Charles Handy himself, the guru who is now backing away from business to study human fulfilment in work and life.

But Hammer goes on to argue that the process-centred world is here and will not go away. 'The question we must confront is not whether to accept it but what we make of it.' And in words that he could never have envisaged in 1994, he claims it can give workers a sense of control and influence which will enhance their lives – even enable them to see their work as a 'service to humanity.'

'In the process-centred world dignity is restored to work, the dignity that was lost to workers who only performed repetitive tasks.'

KEY WRITINGS

Hammer, M. (1990) 'Reengineering Work: Don't Automate, Obliterate', Cambridge, Mass.: *Harvard Business Review* (July/Aug).
Hammer, M. and Champy, J. (1993, 1995) *Reengineering the Corporation*, New York: HarperCollins; London: Nicholas Brealey.
Hammer, M. and Stanton, S. A. (1995) *The Reengineering Revolution*, New York and London: HarperCollins.
Champy, J. (1995) *Reengineering Management*, London: HarperCollins.
Hammer, M. (1996, 1997) *Beyond Reengineering*, New York: HarperBusiness; London: HarperCollins Business.

14

CHARLES HANDY

(b. 1932)

The future of work and organizations

Britain's only world-class business guru and philosopher,
noted for his studies of organizations and his far-reaching
ideas on the future of work and business structures. Since
the publication in 1997 of *The Hungry Spirit*, his most
philosophical work yet, Handy has declared his intention
to draw back from management topics and to concentrate
on wider issues of life, society and individual fulfilment.

Handy was born in Kildare into what he calls 'the
Parnellian tradition,' the son of a southern Irish Protestant
clergyman, and says this background is an important key
to his development: 'it gave me a slightly irreverent
streak and a tendency to ask "why?"'

After graduating from Oriel College, Oxford, with a
First in Greats, Handy worked for Shell International in
Malaysia and as an economist in the City of London and
then spent a formative two years at MIT's Sloan School
of Management. Here he 'sat at the feet' of Warren
Bennis (qv), an authority on organization theory but now
principally associated with leadership, who remains a
good friend and is probably his strongest influence
('Bennis is my godfather'); Ed Schein (qv), the 'career
anchor' guru who became identified with the study of
corporate culture; and Chris Argyris (qv), the organizational psychologist. Douglas McGregor, of Theory X and
Y fame, had recently died, but his ideas still powerfully

76

influenced a group of disciples at MIT.

Handy has said that his experiences working with the Sloan School gurus 'transformed my life.' It was the end of his fledgling career as a businessman; he returned to London to launch and direct the Sloan Management Programme at the newly established London Business School.

From 1977 to 1981 he was Warden of St. George's House in Windsor Castle, a private conference and study centre concerned with issues of ethics and values in society. It was here that he carried out the research for *The Future of Work* (1984), and the appointment marked something of a watershed in his life. Handy went to St. George's instead of joining the church itself, and it enabled him to extend his teaching and thinking beyond business executives and management issues.

Handy's first book *Understanding Organizations* (1976), has become a bible in some quarters and has been revised several times to take account of the vast changes in business cultures that have taken place since the mid-1970s.

His second book, *Gods of Management* (1978), which explored corporate culture in a highly original manner, is his personal favourite: he feels it is his most creative. 'It was before its time,' he says. 'It's still the best way of getting a quick fix on organizations and to find clues on how they need to change.'

It develops an apparently whimsical concept (first sketched out in *Understanding Organizations*) – that all organizations can be classified according to the characteristics of four ancient Greek gods: Zeus (power, patriarchy, the club culture); Apollo (order, reason and bureaucracy, the role culture); Athena (expertise, wisdom, meritocracy, the task culture); and Dionysus (individualism, professional rather than corporate, the existential culture). It is one of the earliest, though underrated, works on company culture.

In the 1980s, Handy turned away from full-time academic work, combining writing and broadcasting with teaching, and thus practising his own blueprint for 'portfolio' living as developed in *The Future of Work*. This stimulating volume threw off scores of ideas around the proposition that lifetime careers are becoming a thing of the past and that those fortunate individuals who are knowledge or brain workers rather than manual workers will in future be able to design a range of jobs for themselves to suit the way they want to spend their time.

The idea had already been touched upon in *Gods of Management* (each of Handy's books in a sense foreshadows the next), and is further elaborated in *The Age of Unreason* (1989, paperback 1990), which Handy regards as his most popular book, vividly encapsulating his principal theories on the implications of change in work and society. It was the first of his books to be published in the United States, and so impressed Robert Horton, then chairman and chief executive of British Petroleum, that he invited Handy to advise the company as a consultant.

Handy's joint study with John Constable of the state of management education, entitled *The Making of Managers* (1988), crystallized a widespread unease about the UK's persistent amateurism and accentuated the need to professionalize management. It led to formation of the Management Charter Initiative, in which several eminent management and professional bodies participated, though the concept of the 'chartered manager' has since become bogged down in arguments over qualifications. Handy's commitment to developing the right calibre of management is directly connected to his belief that managers in the future will no longer be able to rely on the experience of their predecessors to help them make decisions.

'Leaders of tomorrow's businesses will have to be more resourceful and imaginative to enable their businesses to survive,' as an article in *Director* summed it up in September, 1989.

Since the early 1990s, Handy has progressively moved more into non-managerial fields of study, and concerned himself with ethics, values and corporate issues beyond the bottom line. Having broadcast regularly for four years in the BBC's radio 'God-slot', Thought for the Day, he published an anthology of these philosophical reflections under the title of *Waiting for the Mountain to Move* (1991).

The diversity of Handy's interests and activities is evident from his work for the Royal Society for the Encouragement of the Arts, Manufactures and Commerce, more commonly known as the Royal Society of Arts. He was chairman of the RSA 1988-1989 and subsequently vice-chairman, and played a leading role in the RSA's research project into business organizations of the future, 'Tomorrow's Company.'

Handy's last purely management book, *Inside Organizations*, was tied in with a BBC television series in 1991. It offers 21 managerial concepts for application to business problems, and is aimed at first-time managers in all types of organizations. It is supremely accessible in its language, using metaphors and anecdotes rather than technical jargon.

His two most recent books, *The Empty Raincoat* (1994) and *The Hungry Spirit* (1997), reflect his growing concern with the individual's struggle to find personal fulfilment in today's shifting world of uncertain work and short-term careers. He is now reluctant to be described as a 'guru' in its business sense, although happy to think of himself passing on wisdom and ideas to individuals in search of them.

While giving up business consultancy and most paid lecture work, he will be doing more broadcasting of a personal nature, and his next book is planned around individuals who created, like the alchemists of old, something from nothing, whether a business or a social organization.

Charles Handy openly aspires to be numbered among those who 'change the way the world behaves' and who 'affect the way in which managers think.' In this generation his own list of gurus who have achieved such a status would include Drucker, Deming, Bennis, Porter, Peters, Pascale and Mintzberg.

Like Peter Drucker, Handy's eclectic range of interests and wide-angle view of economic and social change make him hard to categorize as a management guru. Drucker has written more on the techniques of management and has nearly 30 years' start on Handy, but both share a curiosity about the directions of society and a gift for extrapolating future trends. (Drucker's *The Age of Discontinuity* did for the 1970s and 1980s what Handy's *The Age of Unreason* may do for the 1990s and early twenty-first century – foreshadow cataclysms of change in industry and economics.)

Certain Handy concepts have remained constant throughout his writing – the increasing shift from lifetime employment in a single company to 'portfolio' work, less secure but more fulfilling; the evolution of new organizational forms such as the 'shamrock' company (a core of essential staff flanked by contract specialists and part-time helpers) and the 'Triple I' (information, intelligence, ideas), in which managers will be required to rise to the challenge of managing knowledge workers, individuals with far different aspirations from the hierarchy-conscious personnel of the past.

Increasingly, he is concerned with how companies manage their goals beyond the pursuit of profit, and whether they can develop into communities of human endeavour rather than properties to be bought and sold in the marketplace. He fears, however, that the Western model of company-as-property will prevail over the eastern model of company-as-community.

For the student of management, business and the organizations that sustain them, Handy's *Understanding Organizations* provides a valuable synthesis of ideas propounded by himself and others. Here you will find explained the major theories of motivation and why we work – the satisfaction theory of Herzberg, the incentive theory of Morse and Weiss, the intrinsic theory of McGregor and Likert (the response of the individual to a worthwhile job).

The book also examines leadership and the culture of organizations, how people behave within them and the power games they play. Handy concludes with a preliminary sketch for his vision of the future organization, which has occupied much of his thinking since, including the changes wrought by communications (fewer people needing to travel physically to their place of work) and leaner organizations paying fees to contract workers rather than salaries and overheads to staff.

Handy says he writes books to clarify his ideas and advises readers of *Understanding Organizations* to 'burn this book after reading it and to write their own – it's the only way to really own the concepts.' It is not, he emphasizes, a book purely for students of business, but concerns organizations of all kinds. He has written separately on schools as organizations and on voluntary organizations.

'Organizations are changing,' he told an interviewer in *Director* magazine in September 1989. 'The days have gone when you went into the kitchens and worked your way up. Soon there won't be promotion prospects after 30. People have got to be prepared to run their own operations – to be competent in all aspects of management.' As the monolithic 'palace' structures of corporations give way, he says memorably, 'we are being thrust into a world of tents.'

In *The Age of Unreason* (his name for the coming era of wrenching change), Handy warns that in the business organization, as in other areas of life, 'the *status quo* will no longer be the best way forward.' To counter the challenge, he recommends a process he calls 'upside-down thinking,' a process not unrelated to Edward de Bono's (qv) 'lateral thinking.' The book shows how the technique can be applied to solving problems of change and, though written for a popular readership, offers stimulating new perspectives to managers and students of management.

The Empty Raincoat (1994), published in the US as *The Age of Paradox*, further developed many of the ideas in *The Age of Unreason*, revealing the hollowness at the heart of economic growth and its impact on human aspirations. The dilemma of greater corporate wealth and fewer jobs that it explored was summed up in the equation offered by the chairman of a large pharmaceutical company: half as many people paid twice as well and producing three times as much, equals productivity and profit. The book ranged widely over changing business and society and was a massive best-seller.

Handy followed it up in 1997 with *The Hungry Spirit*, which focused more on the individual at sea in a bewildering world of change. One or two leading business reviewers criticised its idealistic, philosophical tone and the repetition of many earlier ideas, but Handy was looking for, and achieved, a wider, younger readership than is generally associated with management books.

His reputation as a management thinker remains securely based, however, and his first major work, *Understanding Organizations*, is still much in demand as a classic text.

KEY WRITINGS

Handy, C. (1976, 1991, 1998) *Understanding Organizations*, London: Penguin Books.

Handy C. (1986, 1991) *Gods of Management*, London: Souvenir Press; Business Books.

Handy, C. (1984, 1986) *The Future of Work*, Oxford: Basil Blackwell.

Handy, C. and Constable, J. (1988) *The Making of Managers*, London: Longman.

Handy, C. (1989, 1990) *The Age of Unreason*, London: Business Books; Arrow.

Handy, C. (1990) *Inside Organizations: 21 Ideas for Managers*, London: BBC Books.

Handy, C. (1994) *The Empty Raincoat: Making Sense of the Future*, London: Hutchinson; Boston: Harvard Business School Press (as *The Age of Paradox*).

Handy, C. (1997) *The Hungry Spirit: Beyond Capitalism – A Quest for Purpose in the Modern World*, London: Hutchinson; New York: Broadway.

FREDERICK HERZBERG

(b. 1923)

*'Motivation' and 'maintenance' factors in job
satisfaction*

US clinical psychologist, now professor of management at
the University of Utah, whose work on human motivation separates the elements of a job into those serving
animal or economic needs ('hygiene' or 'maintenance'
factors) and those meeting deeper aspirations ('motivation' factors). Herzberg gives these a timeless context
with Biblical analogies and believes that individual needs
and expectations 'are shaped by the religious/philosophi-
cal system in which one lives.'

More urgently, he relates job satisfaction or dissatisfaction to mental health, and has described his work as
originating in his World War II experiences as a US
army volunteer posted to Dachau concentration camp
after liberation. Here, he 'realized that a society goes
insane when the sane are driven insane.' After the war,
he worked for the US Public Health Service on research
projects, particularly concerning mental illness. Reading
all that had been published on industrial psychology up to
that time, he identified a void in conceptual thinking that
he set out to fill with his behavioural theories.

Herzberg, who coined the concept of 'job enrichment'
to add motivational factors (he says the theory has 'given
employment to a hell of a lot of consultants'), is also one
of the few management thinkers and writers to have
worked at the sharp end of industry as a consultant; in his

case, with the telecommunications giant AT&T. He distilled his thinking about motivation in a 1968 *Harvard Business Review* article – 'One More Time: How Do You Motivate Employees?' which is said to be that journal's biggest selling article, with well over a million reprinted copies sold.

It was Herzberg's 1959 book *The Motivation to Work*, written in collaboration with two research colleagues, B. Mausner and B. B. Snyderman, that established him as an original thinker about the mainsprings of human activity in the workplace. The type of investigation it used has been followed by at least 16 other studies, some in Communist countries, making the original research, in Herzberg's words, 'one of the most replicated studies in the field of job attitudes.'

The *Motivation to Work* was based on intensive questioning of 200 Pittsburgh engineers and accountants, asking them to analyse times when they felt exceptionally good and exceptionally bad about their work. The book was the first to discover that satisfaction and dissatisfaction with one's employment arose from quite different factors and were not simply opposing reactions to the same factors.

The factors that led to feelings of satisfaction, Herzberg found, were 'motivation' ones such as achievement, recognition, satisfaction in the nature of the work itself, responsibility, progress and personal growth (of which the last three were the most important). Dissatisfaction nearly always related to 'hygiene' factors such as company policy, working conditions, salary, status and job security.

'Man has two sets of needs,' explained Herzberg in a later book, *Work and the Nature of Man*; 'his need as an animal to avoid pain and his need as a human to grow psychologically.'

Herzberg illustrates his theory by Biblical example. 'Motivation' is represented by Abraham, made in the image of God and capable of great achievements in self-development; 'hygiene' by Adam, who was faced after the expulsion from Eden with the need to meet bodily requirements – food, warmth, safety, security, avoidance of pain. Both are part of the human condition at work, argues Herzberg, and a lack in one cannot be compensated by fulfilment in the other. 'Animal-Adam' seeks avoidance of pain from the environment or job; 'Human-Abraham' seeks growth and self-realization from tasks. The individual becomes unhappy without the first factor, but it brings only temporary relief, like an analgesic, and the effects soon wear off without deeper satisfactions.

Herzberg's solution was to evolve an 'industrial engineering' philosophy which would design the 'Abraham' factor into jobs. This technique he called 'job enrichment.'

Where it has been done – for example, by enhancing a worker's accountability or by giving him or her additional authority – the changes have brought substantial benefits.

As jobs become 'enriched,' the need for much mundane job supervision disappears, and hitherto unsatisfying supervisory tasks can themselves be enriched by enlarging their responsibilities on a more managerial level.

Herzberg's motivation theories have been reflected in many recent corporate developments such as 'flexitime' and the 'cafeteria' system of choice within a company's benefits system.

KEY WRITINGS

Herzberg, F; Mausner, B. Snyderman, B. (1959) *The Motivation to Work*, New York: Wiley.

Herzberg, F. (1966) *Work and the Nature of Man*, World Publishing.

Herzberg, F. (1968) 'One More Time: How Do You Motivate Employees?' Cambridge, Mass.: *Harvard Business Review*.

Herzberg, F. (1976) *Managerial Choice: To be Efficient and to be Human*, Dow Jones, Irwin.

JOHN HUMBLE

(b. 1925)

*Management by Objectives as a practical
methodology*

British management consultant who took Peter Drucker's concept of Management by Objectives and developed it as a practical tool for managers.

Humble, a Cambridge graduate, is a former director of the old-established consultancy Urwick Orr, whose founder Lyndall Urwick introduced scientific management principles to Britain in the 1920s. Humble has been at the forefront of management development in the UK for many years. In 1967 he joined the Central Training Council of the Department of Employment and later served on the management education committee of the National Economic Development Council. He has also headed consulting teams in many sectors of industry from engineering to retail distribution.

Humble has written or edited half a dozen books. In 1966 he received the British Institute of Management's Burnham Medal 'in recognition of his original work in the area of management objectives.'

The theory of Management by Objectives (MBO) was conceived by Peter Drucker in the 1950s to define the tasks required of the visionary manager, the manager who can see the goals of the business beyond his functional role. Drucker identified eight areas in a business that were suitable for performance objectives: market standing, innovation, productivity, physical and financial resources, profitability, manager performance and development, worker performance and attitude, and public responsibility. Managers also needed, he said, to devise a measuring system for their objectives and a realistic time scale for their achievement.

Every manager from the chairman to the chief clerk needs 'clearly spelled out objectives,' said Drucker. These objectives should set out what each manager's unit is expected to achieve, with the emphasis on teamwork: other units cooperate towards the manager's goals, while his unit in turn helps others to achieve theirs.

'These objectives should always derive from the goals of the business enterprise' and managers needed to be able to measure their performance against these goals, said Drucker.

Drucker called MBO 'a philosophy of management;' John Humble was the first to introduce it to the UK and to develop the philosophy into a practical methodology. He spent three months in the US on a Ford Foundation grant studying best practice in American companies.

Humble defined MBO as 'the attempt to clarify the goals of management objectivity so that the responsibility for achieving the goals was reasonably distributed round the management team, and to check standards of performance against which management effectiveness can be measured.'

The idea of breaking down corporate aims into a series of personal objectives throughout the management team sounds simple but runs the risk of the objectives being too ambitious or too modest to work. Many companies subsequently suffered from too rigid a faith in planning and forecasting and the temptation to pitch their objectives too high without, in the words of a Beecham Group executive, 'legislating for failure.' The reverse danger, of setting objectives too low, tended to be overlooked in Humble's elegant circular structure that moved from strategic planning to tactical planning to unit planning to individual managers' results and back to review, control and strategic planning.

Humble intended to encourage managers throughout the

organization to play 'a creative part' in establishing the standards of performance they would be expected to meet, a sort of continuous self-appraisal mechanism working for the corporate good, and at the same time enhancing personal satisfaction. But, as management writer Robert Heller has pointed out: 'The executive soon catches on to the notion that, if he is being held to a plan or objective, the plan had better be one he can meet.'

MBO in its original form has few adherents today, though elements have been adopted by most successful businesses and strategic planning in particular has an increasingly recognized role in British corporations.

Humble later switched the focus of his work to studying the impact and integration of information technology on business strategy, and in the 1970s concentrated on the often controversial role of the multinational corporation and its responsibilities to the communities in which it operates, particularly in the Third World.

KEY WRITING

Humble, J. W. (1971) *Management By Objectives*, Maidenhead: McGraw-Hill.

ELLIOTT JAQUES

(b. 1917)

Psychological and social factors in group behaviour

Canadian psychologist and doctor of medicine who became a founder member of the Tavistock Institute of Human Relations in London, an organization that did much pioneering work after World War II on the sociology of industry and management. A graduate of both the University of Toronto (BA and MA) and Johns Hopkins Medical School (MD), Jaques served as a major in the Royal Canadian Army Medical Corps between 1941 and 1945.

Jaques's principal fame rests on his work in studying the psychological and social factors behind group behaviour, first carried out at the Glacier Metal Company in London. He also developed a theory of measuring the value of work by the time span of 'discretion' that elapses before decisions are monitored.

From the mid-1960s to the mid-1980s Jaques was associated with Brunel University in Uxbridge, Middlesex, as head of the School of Social Science (1965-70) and director of the university's Institute of Organization and Social Studies (1970–85). He has been a government adviser to the Board of Trade on overseas marketing and on the reorganization of the National Health Service. Jaques retired from Brunel in 1985 and since 1989 has been visiting research professor of management sciences at George Washington University, Washington, D.C.

Elliott Jaques' studies in worker behaviour at the Glacier Metal Company, carried out between 1948 and 1965, were at least a decade ahead of their time and remain the most extensive of their kind to be carried out on the factory floor. The 'working-through' process he pioneered, using an investigator interacting with a group on its problems, uncovered, most importantly, the need that workpeople feel to have their role and status defined in a way that they and their colleagues can accept. Confusion of roles or unclear boundaries of responsibility lead to frustration and insecurity, and to a tendency in management to avoid authority and accountability.

Jaques' work on wage problems at Glacier Metal led to him formulating a theory of the value of different types of work, based on 'the time-span of discretion' – the length of time that elapses before the actions or decision of an individual worker are monitored by superiors. The lowest-paid workers tend to have their actions monitored at frequent intervals, whereas high-level decisions may take years to be evaluated. This resulted in a book called *The Measurement of Responsibility* in 1956, five years after his ground-breaking Glacier investigations were published as *The Changing Culture of a Factory*. (Jaques also collaborated with the managing director of Glacier Metal, Wilfred Brown, on the *Glacier Project Papers* in 1965.)

Jaques later developed a theory of bureaucracy in which progression up an organization, with increasing levels of discretion, was not viewed in relation to a simple chronological time-span, but as seven main strata defined by length of service: up to three months; up to one year; two years; five years; ten years, 20 years and more than 20 years. These were the levels at which pay differentials were accepted as being fair. Jaques maintains that any rational pay policy would be accepted as just if differences between these discretionary levels were properly worked out first.

In *A General Theory of Bureaucracy*, Jaques also examines the different perceptions of a worker when asked to describe his boss. He may see his 'real' boss – the one from whom he feels he has a chance of getting a decision about himself – as someone quite different from the person next in line up the hierarchy.

Jaques quotes from military staff example to illustrate that real decisions are never made in the way they are supposed to be made in the hierarchy charts. 'They would all be killed while trying to sort out who was giving orders to whom.' He concludes from this and bureaucratic example in Eastern Europe (of the 1970s) 'that it is never possible to tell from an organization chart just who is manager of whom: in effect, it is a wise manager (or subordinate) who knows his own subordinate (or manager).'*

•

KEY WRITINGS

Jaques, E. (1951) *The Changing Culture of a Factory*, London: Tavistock.

Jaques, E. (1956) *The Measurement of Responsibility*, London: Tavistock.

Brown, W. and Jaques, E. (1965) *Glacier Project Papers*, London: Heinemann.

Jaques, E. (1961, 1967) *Equitable Payment*, London: Heinemann; Penguin Books.

Jaques, E. (1976) *A General Theory of Bureaucracy*, London: Heinemann.

Jaques, E. (1982) *Free Enterprise, Fair Employment*, London: Hienemann.

Jacques, E. (1989) *Requisite Organisation*, London: Gower.

*E. Jaques. *A General Theory of Bureaucracy* (Heinemann, 1976), quoted in *Organization Theory*, ed D. S. Pugh (Penguin, 1990)

JOSEPH M. JURAN

(b. 1904)

Company-wide quality cannot be delegated

US electrical engineer, born in Romania, who worked contemporaneously with W. Edwards Deming (qv) on pioneering the quality management revolution that began in postwar Japan. Ironically, no industrialist in the US was interested in the theories of Deming and Juran – the production mentality ruled at the time – until Japanese manufacturing, practising the quality philosophy, began driving American products to the wall.

By coincidence, both Deming and Juran had become interested in the techniques of assuring quality in manufacturing based on statistical control while working in the 1920s at Western Electric, the manufacturing division of Bell Telephone System. Juran joined Western in 1924, three years before the famous Elton Mayo (qv) experiments at Western's Hawthorne plant in Chicago, which revolutionized thinking about motivation and the human element in industry. Here he worked with the brilliant statistician Walter A. Shewhart, who developed a method for controlling quality in manufacturing.

Juran then joined the manufacturing side of AT&T in the 1920s. He became a corporate industrial engineer and later branched out as a quality consultant.

He articulated precise steps for achieving consistent quality, and was the first to define the Pareto Principle, named for the Italian economist Vilfredo Pareto (1848-

1923), who discovered that most wealth in a nation is concentrated in the hands of a few people while the majority are relatively poor. Juran refined this to the now-familiar 80-20 division in which, for example, 20 per cent of a company's products generate 80 per cent of its revenue, or in which 80 per cent of sales come from 20 per cent of the sales force.

Juran established his reputation in 1951 with the publication of his *Quality Control Handbook*, the first manual of its kind. The Japanese, who had already absorbed Deming's lessons to the extent of instituting a Deming Prize that year, invited Juran to Tokyo in 1953 for a series of lectures. In the early 1980s his contribution to Japanese quality achievements was recognized with the award of the Order of the Sacred Treasure, second class, an honour also conferred on Deming.

Since 1954 he has preached his gospel in Japan and claims some of the credit for turning round Japan's initially poor reputation for quality. His 'Management of Quality' courses have been attended by more than 20,000 managers in over 30 countries. As a consultant, his clients include Texas Instruments, Du Pont, Monsanto, Xerox, Motorola and the Internal Revenue Service.

Juran's principal contribution to quality management thinking is his methodology for determining the avoidable and the unavoidable costs of quality, thus providing a yardstick for measuring the cost of a quality programme.

Juran has devised a structured concept known as CWQM – Company-Wide Quality Management. He believes it absolutely essential for senior managers to involve themselves, to define the goals, to assign responsibilities and to measure progress. Quality, Juran teaches, cannot be delegated.

Like other management thinkers – notably Peter Drucker (qv), Charles Handy (qv) and Rosabeth Moss Kanter (qv) – Juran has developed a vision of the future corporation, in which he sees quality targets being incorporated in business plans as routinely as targets for sales, profits, return on capital and earnings per share. Like Moss Kanter, Juran sees greater 'empowerment' of the workforce as a key – in this case to achieving quality through self-organization and self-supervision. For Juran, quality has always been indissolubly linked with human relations and teamwork.

Joseph M. Juran and W. Edwards Deming are so closely linked – by age, experience and their part in the Japanese economic miracle – that it is sometimes hard to differentiate their contributions. Juran himself has set out to develop Company-Wide Quality Management into a full-blown corporate philosophy, and has criticized the Deming approach for being more at home with statistics than with management.

Juran's approach is heavily oriented towards the human side of achieving quality, and he has praised the Japanese use of quality circles for their effect on human relations in the workplace, while acknowledging that QCs have accounted for less than ten per cent of Japan's improvement in quality.

The Juran methodology was clearly laid out in *Juran on Planning for Quality* (1988), which set out to demonstrate how quality planning affects different levels of company activity. It outlined the Juran 'quality trilogy' – quality planning, quality management and quality improvement – by which managers learn how to implement strategic quality planning across the company.

Key elements include: identifying customers and their needs; creating measurements of quality; planning processes that are capable of meeting quality goals under operating conditions; producing continuing improvements in market share and premium prices and in reducing the error rate.

The book emphasized the universal application of quality commitment throughout an organization – to all products, both goods and services; to all corporate levels from CEO downwards; to all corporate functions from general management to product development: and to all industries, in both the manufacturing and service sectors.

Juran continued to publish books on aspects of quality planning and design into his late eighties, and at the age of

92 was working on a five-volume autobiography. A recommended recent biography is *Juran: A Lifetime of Influence*, by John Butman (John Wiley, New York, 1997).

KEY WRITINGS

Juran, J. M. (1951) *Quality Control Handbook*, New York: McGraw-Hill.
Juran, J. M. (1988) *Juran on Planning for Quality*, New York: Free Press; London: Collier Macmillan.
Juran, J. M. (1989) *Juran on Leadership for Quality: An Executive Handbook*, New York: Free Press.
Juran, J. M. (1992) *Juran on Quality by Design*, New York: Free Press.

ROSABETH MOSS KANTER

(b. 1943)

The 'post-entrepreneurial' corporation: empowering
individuals as a force for change

US sociologist, professor of business administration at
Harvard and former editor of the *Harvard Business Review*,
who has established herself as a leading authority on managing change, developing the 'post-entrepreneurial' corporation and 'empowering' human potential in organizations.
She is now one of the most sought-after consultants in the
US (clients include IBM, CBS, Procter & Gamble,
Honeywell, Digital, Apple, Xerox and General Electric)
and a celebrated TV performer on both sides of the
Atlantic. A BBC television documentary described her as
'a fearless critic of management tradition.'

Born in Cleveland, Ohio, Moss Kanter graduated from
the élite female academy Bryn Mawr and took her Ph.D.
at the University of Michigan, later joining the faculty of
Brandeis University as associate professor of sociology
before moving to Harvard in 1973. Between 1977 and
1986 she taught at Yale and MIT before returning to
Harvard as professor of business administration. In 1988
she worked as a key economic adviser to Michael
Dukakis in his campaign for the Presidency against
George Bush.

Kanter's award-winning first book, *Men and Women of
the Corporation* (1977) analysed the bureaucratic factors
that locked people into pre-determined roles in a code-
named industrial corporation, and how this prevented the

business from fully tapping the talent within it.

The Change Masters (1983) compared the characteristics of such change-resisters with those of innovative corporations which stimulated entrepreneurship within themselves and became market leaders. Combining as it did the academic discipline of Kanter's background in organizational sociology with her hands-on experience as a consultant in industry, the book was hailed as 'the thinking manager's *In Search of Excellence.*'

When Giants Learn to Dance (1989) in effect completed a trilogy on the deep changes facing corporate America. Kanter examined a broad range of corporations, large and small, working from the inside on consulting projects, and found that very different organizations were converging towards similar solutions to the problems of competing in the new global 'corporate Olympics.'

The new model corporation Kanter outlines is 'post-entrepreneurial' – lean and athletic with fewer management levels, able to 'do more with less,' to anticipate change and open itself up to opportunities such as strategic alliances with other companies. A focal point of the corporate Olympic runner is to achieve synergies, where the whole is worth more than the sum of its parts; Kanter's inside studies of merger and acquisition strategy and culture change are particularly fascinating.

The last third of the book studies the impact of the post-entrepreneurial organization on the people who work in it. The implications for careers (from climbing the corporate ladder to developing portable 'employability'), for pay (as determinants switch from position to performance, from status to contribution), and for the psychological wellbeing of individuals are all explored with stimulating intellectual zeal. The trilogy thus in a sense comes full circle, focusing on the key task of managing the creative potential of the men and women of the corporation as corporate reality changes about them.

The book achieved both intellectual and popular status within a short time: Tom Peters has described it as 'the benchmark against which management books of the nineties are measured.'

Rosabeth Moss Kanter has pursued a logical progression from studying how traditional, bureaucratic organizations stultify individual talents to identifying how the 'post-entrepreneurial' corporation is releasing and 'empowering' those talents in flatter, less hierarchical structures.

Men and Women of the Corporation, which won a US award in 1977 for the best book on social issues, discovered that the highest value placed on managers was 'predict-ability.' Women, whether in the traditional roles of secretaries or company wives (with all their potential for influence in the corporation) were regarded as both unpredictable and incomprehensible.

Kanter's research for this book led her to conclude that there was crucial need for change in the average industrial corporation in order to improve the quality of working life, to create equal employment opportunities for men, women and minority groups, and to enable employees to make better use of their talents to the benefit of the corporation. To achieve this, she perceived that the following changes in organizational structure would be required:

1. Management should be opened up to promotion from a wider range of candidates, including women and hith-erto powerless individuals like clerical workers. Changes in certain areas, such as systems of appraisal and career development, would be needed to achieve this. Intermediate jobs would need to be created to bridge these jobs with management.
2. Empowering strategies would be necessary, leading to a flatter hierarchy, decentralized authority and autonomous work groups.

Building on her discoveries about resistance to change, Kanter's second book studied in depth leading companies that could be defined as 'change masters,' illuminating the factors that encourage innovation as a way of life, and the problems that the search for innovation brings in its wake. Kanter's principal discovery was that firms prone to inno-vate have an 'integrative' approach to problems and a will-ingness to challenge established practices; to judge a course of action by a vision of the future rather than by the accepted ways of the past. Firms unlikely to innovate were typically 'segmentalist' in approach, compartmented by department and unable to see problems whole.

Throughout *The Change Masters*, Kanter argued that the key to a corporate renaissance was 'participation management' or empowerment – making possible the mechanisms by which individuals could contribute their ideas. It is only in integrative companies that individuals can improve their leverage, thus contributing to their own and the corporate success.

When Giants Learn to Dance (1989) extends this philosophy to the future shape and character of the globally competitive corporation, which she describes as 'post-entrepreneurial . . . applying entrepreneurial principles to the giant corporation' in order to make it flexible and responsive to change while maintaining a disciplined efficiency – combining 'the power of an elephant with the agility of a dancer.' In the aftermath of the 'excellence' era, she suggests, companies are facing some problems not addressed by Peters and Waterman, such as 'Who has the power to start or block innovations?' and 'Who gets the financial returns?'

Kanter's detailed and knowledgeable case studies suggest that companies as different as, for example, Eastman Kodak and Apple Computers, are increasingly converging towards similar solutions when faced with the challenge of competing in the global 'corporate Olympics.' Her practical experience as a consultant comes through in such examples of the new strategy as 'the corporation as switchboard', where comparatively small head offices manage a network of other organizations, or contract out former company services as market-oriented businesses. (A crucial byproduct of the latter, essential to Kanter's argument, is that staffs are no longer considered as 'overhead' but as potential sources of value.)

Much of the book is devoted to the study of achieving synergy and all the components required for it, including the flatter management structure which enables greater cooperation across divisions and departments.

Another key idea is encapsulated in the acronym PAL – '*pool* resources with others, *ally* to exploit an opportunity or *link* systems in a partnership.' Companies can become better PALs with suppliers, venture partners, service contractors, customers and unions. In purchasing, for example, they shed the adversarial character of earlier practice, when the prevailing wisdom was to minimize price by maintaining a large vendor base and insisting on short-term contracts. The growth of joint ventures as a means of access to foreign markets has contributed strongly to the new ethos.

Kanter's keen perception of the individual human dimension within organizations leads her to identify the dangers in becoming more 'mean' than 'lean' and to stress, on a personal level, the importance of shared values in the corporation.

The impact of post-entrepreneurialism on individual careers, with rewards linked more to contribution than to position or status, and with a more flexible structure bringing an end to the lifetime career ladder, is fully explored. Management, for its part, becomes even more complex and demanding when it switches from the mentality of boss to that of partner.

Empowering the individual within the company, which this implies, has been a Kanter preoccupation for years. In 1979, her *Harvard Business Review* article 'Power Failures in Management Circuits' (*HBR* July/August 1979) identified those organizational factors affecting individuals which create power or powerlessness to influence events and people, e.g. discretion, recognition, relevance to central problems, sponsors, peer networks and subordinates.

'The powerless live in a different world . . . they may turn instead to the ultimate weapon of those who lack productive power – oppressive power . . . .' This she identified as a prime cause of dissatisfaction with frontline supervisors, a category especially subject to the feeling of powerlessness. Staff professionals and isolated top executives are other susceptible categories, leading in Kanter's view to conservatism and resistance to change in those areas. Women managers experience particular failures of power, she found, because organizations are geared to employing them in routine, low-profile jobs.

Kanter's key message here is: 'By empowering others, a leader does not decrease his power; instead, he may increase it – especially if the whole organization performs better.'

Her seven essential skills for managers of the future, set out in *When Giants Learn to Dance*, are:

- Learn to operate without the hierarchy 'crutch'
- Know how to compete in a way that enhances, not undercuts, co-operation
- Operate to the highest ethical standards
- Possess a dose of humility
- Develop a process focus on how things are done
- Be multi-faceted and ambidextrous, work across functions to find synergies
- Be able to gain satisfaction from results and be willing to stake your own rewards on them

Kanter's post-entrepreneurial model corporation is a three-part mix: the values and goals emanating from top management; the channels, forums, programmes and relationships designed in the middle to support those goals and values; and the project ideas bubbling up from below – 'ideas for new ventures or technological innovations, or better ways to serve customers.'

Like other leading gurus, Kanter has turned her attention to globalization and in *World Class* (1995) she examines how the global economy, with its vast expansion of customer choice, is transforming companies of all sizes and the communities in which they operate. It is the best book yet on globalization and what it means in practice to the future of businesses. In a fascinating microcosm, she presents a variation on Michael Porter's 'cluster' theory of industrial success, showing how the city of Boston reinvented itself from a decaying centre of manufacturing to a hive of world-class technology and knowledge businesses, feeding off and reinforcing the city's fabled centres of educational excellence such as Harvard University and Massachusetts Institute of Technology with its leading-edge Media Lab.

Many of Kanter's most influential writings, including the

'Power Circuits' article from *Harvard Business Review* in 1979, were collected in 1997 in *Rosabeth Moss Kanter on the Frontiers of Management* (Harvard Business School Press).

Her books deserve careful and thoughtful reading: their many-faceted ideas resist easy categorization and will play a shaping role in management theory for years to come.

KEY WRITINGS

Kanter, R. M. (1977) *Men and Women of the Corporation*, Basic Books.

Kanter, R. M. (1983, 1984) *The Change Masters: Corporate Entrepreneurs at Work*, New York: Simon and Schuster; London: Allen & Unwin.

Kanter, R. M. (1989) *When Giants Learn to Dance*, New York and London: Simon & Schuster; (1998) London: International Thomson Business Press.

Kanter, R. M. (1979) 'Power Failures in Management Circuits', Cambridge, Mass.: *Harvard Business Review*; reprinted in *Organization Theory*, (1990) ed. D. S. Pugh, London: Penguin Books.

Kanter, R. M. (1992) *The Challenge of Organizational Change*, New York: Simon and Schuster.

Kanter, R. M. (1995) *World Class: Thriving Locally in the Global Economy*, New York: Simon and Schuster.

Kanter, R. M. (1997) *Rosabeth Moss Kanter on the Frontiers of Management*, Boston: Harvard Business School Press.

ROBERT S. KAPLAN AND DAVID P. NORTON

(b. 1940) (b. 1941)

The balanced scorecard system of performance measurement

The partnership that invented the 'Balanced Business Scorecard,' a new kind of performance-measurement tool which allows businesses to measure their non-financial as well as financial results, covering such 'soft' but essential areas as customer satisfaction, quality and product cycle times and effectiveness of new product development.

Robert Kaplan is Marvin Bower Professor of Leadership Development at Harvard Business School and has also held a chair of accounting there. He has been on the Harvard faculty since 1984 and before that spent 16 years on the faculty of the Graduate School of Industrial Administration at Carnegie-Mellon University, serving as dean from 1977 to 1983.

A graduate in electrical engineering from Massachusetts Institute of Technology, with a doctorate in operations research from Cornell University, Kaplan has received a number of awards for outstanding contributions to the accountancy profession. His research, teaching and consulting work all focus on new cost and performance measurement systems, primarily activity-based costing and the balanced scorecard. He has authored or co-authored more than 100 academic papers and nine books.

David Norton is president and CEO of Renaissance Solutions, Inc., an international consultancy firm specializing in performance measurement and organizational renewal. Before Renaissance, he co-founded Nolan Norton and Company, where he spent 17 years as president before the firm's acquisition by Peat Marwick. He is a Harvard DBA (doctor of business administration) and, like his colleague Kaplan, earned his first degree in electrical engineering.

The balanced scorecard concept had its genesis when the two men worked together in 1990 on a one-year multi-company study called 'Measuring Performance in the Organization of the Future.' The study was carried out by Norton's old company, which had been renamed the Nolan Norton Institute and was the research arm of the accountancy and consulting giant KPMG. Norton was the study leader and Kaplan an academic consultant. Also participating were representatives of a dozen companies, from manufacturing and service industries, both heavy-duty and high-tech. All had come to believe that financial performance measurements were no longer enough to enable a company to remain competitive and enhance its economic value.

As Kaplan and Norton explain in the preface to their book *The Balanced Scorecard: Translating Strategy into Action* (1996), a number of innovative case studies on performance measurement were reviewed early in the project, among them a new type of 'corporate scorecard' from Analog Devices that contained, in addition to traditional financial measures, others on customer delivery times, quality and cycle times of manufacturing processes and effectiveness of new product development. Analog also had a system for measuring continuous improvement processes.

Group discussions of the scorecard expanded it into four main quadrants: financial, customer, innovation and internal/learning development. The name 'balanced scorecard' was chosen to reflect the balance between long and short-term objectives, financial and non-financial, lagging and leading indicators and external and internal performance.

Several companies participating in the research team tried it out in pilot schemes and reported back on its working. By the end of 1991 Kaplan and Norton were ready to summarize the group's findings in a *Harvard Business Review* article ('The Balanced Scorecard – Measures That Drive Performance,' Jan/Feb 1992). It soon became one of the most requested *HBR* reprints, and a new management tool was born.

When Norton became CEO in 1993 of the newly formed Renaissance Solutions, the scorecard was introduced as a vehicle for helping companies translate and implement strategy. An alliance between Renaissance and the much bigger Gemini Consulting brought it into use in major corporate transformations, and further refined the concept to tie measures together in strategic linkages. This meant that it was possible to tell how current investment or other decisions in one area would impact on another and eventually affect the bottom line.

The balanced scorecard is now widely used in US commerce and industry – oil giant Mobil regards it as 'an irreplaceable agenda for discussion of business strategies, strengths, weaknesses and performance' – and its adherents in Europe include some of the UK's major corporations, among them NatWest Bank, British Petroleum and Rolls-Royce Aerospace Group.

The Balanced Business Scorecard has become indispensable in large companies undergoing radical change programmes, because it measures previously hard-to-quantify activities that are increasingly seen as giving a business its competitive edge – such as customer satisfaction and the building of organizational and employee skills.

The rapidly growing awareness that companies must continuously improve or fall by the wayside has given the scorecard an enormous advantage over traditional performance measurements. Historically, these were concerned with financial results and the meeting of targets, but at best they could only provide a snapshot of past performance, not a reliable indicator of how a company might be expected to continue to perform in the future.

As Kaplan explained: 'The financial measures of the most recent period of performance will tell you something about how well that company operated during that period. But there may be processes that they developed during that period for new products or new capabilities that will create long-term value that have yet to show up in the financial statements. And conversely, some organizations may have cut back on some of those investments in capability; in the short run this will make their financial performance look better, but in the process they have mortgaged their future.'

Kaplan and Norton's recognition that companies needed non-financial indicators of future performance as much as financial measures of past performance to survive in a climate of virtually permanent change has brought the Balanced Business Scorecard to the forefront of techniques of change management in the 1990s. Being non-prescriptive and endlessly adaptable, the scorecard can be tailored to any combination of indicators required for a specific business. Its ability to project the impact of business decisions on the company's financial future has also moved it from being primarily a measurement system to a core management system. It is still evolving in the field, and Kaplan and Norton describe the book that followed their three *HBR* articles as 'a progress report.'

The basic principles of the Balanced Business Scorecard are simple. Essentially it looks at a business from four perspectives to gain answers to four key questions:

- The customer perspective: how do our customers see us?
- The internal business perspective: which processes and competencies do we need to excel at?
- Innovation and learning perspective: can we continue to improve and excel?
- Financial perspective: how do we look to our shareholders?

Within these four perspectives, the company decides its objectives and progress towards these objectives is then tracked through specific measures and through initiatives for continuous improvement. The first stage of designing a scorecard is always to formulate a vision or mission statement to drive the objectives. At NatWest, for example, it was 'To be first choice in our chosen markets.' The senior executive management team then works together to translate its corporate strategy into specific strategic objectives. In the customer perspective, for example, it must be specific about its targeted customers and the market segments where it hopes to compete. It should also, in Norton's words, 'look at the world through the eyes of the customer.'

The process of designing a scorecard should take about 16 weeks, though Norton admitted in a 1997 interview that he had 'yet to find an executive team with a complete consensus about building a scorecard.' In less than 50 per cent of companies, he added, was there even consensus about why customers dealt with that company.

Scorecards can be used at all levels of an organization so that there is alignment between what top management and frontline employees understand is important. In some organizations, Norton has reported, employees walk about with their personal scorecards and describe how their own objectives relate to the corporate ones.

This accessibility to all levels of the organization is crucial to the successful use of the scorecard system, say its originators. 'Frontline employees must understand the financial consequences of their decisions and actions; senior executives must understand the drivers of long-term financial success.' The balanced scorecard is not the only performance measurement system to use non-financial criteria, as Kaplan and Norton are the first to admit. But what it does better than any other system, they would claim, is to translate 'a business unit's mission and strategy into tangible objectives and measures.'

KEY WRITINGS

Kaplan, R. S. and Norton, D. P. (1992) 'The Balanced

Scorecard: Measures That Drive Performance', Cambridge, Mass.: *Harvard Business Review* (Jan/Feb).

Kaplan, R. S. and Norton, D. P. (1993) 'Putting the Balanced Scorecard to Work', Cambridge, Mass.: *Harvard Business Review* (Sept/Oct).

Kaplan, R. S. and Norton, D. P. (1996) *The Balanced Scorecard: Translating Strategy Into Action*, Boston: Harvard Business School Press.

21

PHILIP KOTLER

(b. 1931)

Marketing as a management science

Chicago-born economist, mathematician and sociologist who became the world's leading authority on marketing as an applied discipline capable of raising awareness not only of products and services but of ideas, places, individuals and organizations. His *Marketing Management*, first published in 1967 and currently (1998) in its ninth edition, is the bible of every business school's marketing course. It defined marketing as a function of management and applied a scientific rigour, with models and statistical analysis, to what had been up till then largely a seat-of-the-pants practice, directed largely at selling.

At a New York seminar in the 1980s, Kotler was approached by a businessman who reproached him for America's trials at the hands of Japanese competitors. 'Deming taught quality to the Japanese and you taught them marketing,' said the man. 'The combination defeated us.' Kotler later examined how Japan had mastered global marketing in *The New Competition* (1985).

Kotler trained as an economist and mathematician, taking a master's in economics at the University of Chicago (where he studied under Milton Friedman) in the early 1950s and a PhD at the Massachusetts Institute of Technology under Paul Samuelson, the Nobel laureate. The opposing theories of the free-marketeer Friedman and the Keynesian Samuelson so frustrated him that he quit economics for a post-doctoral year in sociology and a programme in higher mathematics at Harvard. It was here that he met several professors of marketing and became convinced that marketing deserved a more analytical approach.

In 1962 he joined the faculty of Northwestern University, Illinois, where he is now S.C. Johnson and Son Distinguished Professor of International Marketing at the respected J. L. Kellogg Graduate School of Management. He was offered an assistant professorship in either managerial economics or marketing and chose, he says with typical dry humour, 'to teach the subject that I knew less about, namely marketing.'

Existing marketing textbooks seemed to him short on the kind of research and methodology that were common in other disciplines, so he decided to write his own. After his publishers persuaded him to leave out the more daunting academic models and statistics, *Marketing Management* was an immediate success. Four years later, in 1971, he included the excised material in *Marketing Decision Making: A Model-Building Approach*, which was incorporated by the University of Chicago in its introductory marketing course.

In 1969 Kotler and a colleague, Sidney Levy, began to broaden out the study of marketing to non-business uses, and he has since published books applying marketing to subjects as diverse as healthcare organizations, educational institutions, celebrities, performing arts bodies, museums, towns and cities seeking investment and most recently, entire nations.

Though a distinguished academic, Kotler has the knack of distilling the essence of his work in simple concepts: that marketing is basically a matter of exchange in different contexts; that it is 'the art of creating genuine customer value' and of 'filling needs profitably.'

He has updated his masterwork every three years or so and likes to joke that only the most current edition is correct because marketing moves so fast that 'the answers of yesterday lead to the errors of today.'

His current seminars stress such themes as relationship

marketing, speed as a competitive weapon and the role of superior IT systems. In the mid-1980s he took issue with the eminent Theodore Levitt (qv), the first management thinker to treat marketing seriously. Levitt had argued that companies should pursue standardized global products and marketing messages, emulating big brands like Coca Cola and McDonalds. Kotler argued that this was to ignore crucial differences in culture, tastes, income, distribution and many other factors. His approach was 'think global but also local' – a concept now known as 'glocal.'

Kotler continues to teach, consult and run seminars alongside a prolific writing programme (15 books, many co-authored, and over 100 articles in leading management reviews). In 1985 the American Marketing Association made him the first recipient of its Distinguished Marketing Educator award. In accepting it, Kotler said: 'Marketing is not the art of finding clever ways to dispose of what you make. Marketing is the art of creating genuine customer value. It is the art of helping your customers become better off. The marketer's watchwords are quality, service and value. Can you imagine what the world would be like if the marketing concept became a universal principle?'

Before the 1960s, marketing was not seen as a serious function of strategic management, more as a grubby commercial business left to the sales department. That changed in 1960 with the publication of an article in *Harvard Business Review* by Theodore Levitt ('Marketing Myopia', *HBR* July/August 1960) and four years later Philip Kotler began work on the classic textbook that would launch a thousand marketing courses – *Marketing Management: Analysis, Planning, Implementation and Control*, to give its full title, now in its ninth (1997) edition.

Marketing Management broke entirely new ground from the existing lightweight books on the subject. It was divided into six main sections and 26 sub-sections covering every aspect of planning and managing the marketing function, from the societal, managerial and strategic underpinnings of marketing theory and practice, through analysing consumer and organizational buyers to evaluating and controlling market performance.

As befitted its author's polymathic background in economics, mathematics and sociology, it was grounded in decision theory, organizational behaviour, economic science and social psychology and was quickly adopted by Stanford, Wharton and other leading US business schools. Since then, MBAs around the world have been trained on Kotler's teaching that the customer is paramount and that successful companies don't just sell but build relationships with targeted customers and deliver satisfaction to them.

'Authentic marketing is not the art of selling what you make but knowing what to make,' he wrote in the book's introduction. 'It is the art of identifying and understanding customer needs and creating solutions that deliver satisfaction to the customers, profits to the producers, and benefits for the stakeholders. Market leadership is gained by creating customer satisfaction through product innovation, product quality, and customer service. If these are absent, no amount of advertising, sales promotion, or salesmanship can compensate.'

If the core concept of economics is scarcity, that of politics is power and that of sociology is the group, then the core concept of marketing, Kotler argues, is exchange – the exchange of values between two parties. Marketing thus becomes a social process, composed of human behaviour patterns, not merely a function of adding to business profits. This humanistic view led Kotler to broaden out the study of marketing into non-business activities, including the marketing of individuals, cities and even countries. He believes that it is his work on this, rather than his classic textbook, that ranks among the most important marketing milestones of the 1960s because it enabled him to 'take marketing into new sectors of society and show its potential contributions.'

The idea that marketing had a role in non-profitmaking organizations was controversial when Kotler first aired it in

1969 in an article with Sidney Levy in the *Journal of Marketing*, but within two years it had become accepted by fellow-academics. Kotler followed this in 1971 with another controversial breakout from conventional thinking, collaborating with Gerald Zaltman on 'Social Marketing: An Approach to Planned Social Change,' which extended the concept into new, political territory. A third contentious publication was 'Demarketing – Yes, Demarketing,' in *Harvard Business Review* in 1971, based on Kotler's and Levy's observations that some firms actively discourage some customers and encourage others, and advancing the idea that companies and indeed society can use marketing theory in reverse to dampen excessive or socially undesirable demand.

Books with various co-authors poured out on marketing in non-business contexts: *Marketing for Non-Profit Organizations* (1975, 5th edition 1996); *Strategic Marketing for Educational Institutions* (1985, 1995); *Marketing for Healthcare Organizations* (1987); *High Visibility* (1987, 1997), on celebrity marketing; and a raft of others on cultural organizations, hospitality, tourism, the performing arts. In 1993 Kotler published *Marketing Places: Attracting Investment, Industry and Tourism to Cities, States and Nations*, and in 1997 *The Marketing of Nations: A Strategic Approach to Building National Wealth*. In 1986 he advanced the concept of 'Megamarketing,' using political skills and understanding of public opinion to break into blocked or protected markets.

Kotler has identified a number of different levels at which marketing operates, from the lowest level of selling up through targeting specific groups and needs to anticipating needs and finally shaping demand by extending and creating new lifestyles through innovation, such as Sony achieved with the Walkman.

All his work has the common theme that organizations compete for customers and cannot succeed by trying to satisfy all segments; they must select and focus on well defined target groups whose needs they understand. Marketing, he argues, must match the organization's supply capabilities to appropriate market opportunities.

Throughout his career Kotler has been driven by a love

of problem-solving and working out concepts to completion. In a paper circulated privately to one of his classes, he was quoted as saying: 'I operate on the assumption that "progress" is possible, even in the face of much contradictory evidence. I prefer to believe that human beings can improve their condition by applying collective intelligence to solving shared problems.'

KEY WRITINGS

Kotler, P. (1967, 1997) *Marketing Management: Analysis, Planning, Implementation and Control*, Englewood Cliffs, N.J.: Prentice Hall.

Kotler, P. and Levy, S. J. (1969) 'Broadening the Concept of Marketing', *Journal of Marketing* (January).

Kotler, P. and Zaltman, G. (1971) 'Social Marketing: An Approach to Planned Social Change', *Journal of Marketing* (July).

Kotler, P. and Levy, S. J. (1971) 'Demarketing – Yes, Demarketing', Cambridge, Mass.: *Harvard Business Review* (Nov/Dec).

Kotler, P. and Lilien, G. (1971, 1983) *Marketing Decision-Making: A Model-Building Approach*, New York: Holt Rinehart and Winston; 1992, 1996 revised as *Marketing Models*, Englewood Cliffs, N.J: Prentice Hall.

Kotler, P. (1980, 1996) *Principles of Marketing*, Englewood Cliffs, N.J.: Prentice Hall.

Kotler, P. (1986) 'Megamarketing', *Harvard Business Review* (March/April).

Kotler, P. (1987, 1997) *Marketing – An Introduction*, *Englewood Cliffs*, N.J.: Prentice Hall.

Kotler, P. and Roberto, E. (1989) *Social Marketing: Strategies for Changing Social Behavior*, New York: Free Press.

JOHN P. KOTTER

(b. 1947)

Leadership and organizational change

Harvard professor whose work since the early 1980s has focused on managerial qualities and behaviour and is now predominantly associated with the leadership of organizations. Like Warren Bennis (qv), the elder statesman among leadership gurus, he has made detailed studies of what differentiates leaders from managers, with a substantial body of casework that began with his first, much-praised 1982 book *The General Managers*.

Where the two differ is that Bennis, 22 years Kotter's senior, has studied individuals across a variety of occupations in attempting to identify common principles of leadership, while Kotter sets his research firmly in a corporate framework and argues that leadership is a 'process' that sets off hundreds or thousands of 'leadership acts' within the organization.

Kotter's 1990 book, *A Force for Change: How Leadership Differs from Management*, demonstrates this process in action in businesses such as NCR, American Express and SAS. The message of *A Force for Change*, one that Bennis has also expressed, is that thousands of companies are over-managed and under-led because too few executives, while managerially competent, have a clear understanding of what leadership is. Both Kotter and Bennis believe that while leadership qualities may be inherent in some, they can also be imbibed and taught.

Since 1990, Kotter has held the Konosuke Matsushita chair of leadership at Harvard Business School, endowed by the Japanese entrepreneur who founded the giant electrical engineering firm. In 1997 he published a study of Matsushita, one of the most charismatic business leaders Japan has produced, under the title *Matsushita Leadership: Lessons from the 20th Century's Most Remarkable Entrepreneur*, which provided a rare insight into the arcane world of Japanese business philosophy. Kotter's half-dozen other books on leadership are highly regarded, along with *Corporate Culture and Performance* (1992), in which, with co-author James L. Heskett, he analysed the factors common to successful change programmes in large companies – most of them, unsurprisingly, linked to strong and committed leadership.

A graduate (in electrical engineering) of Massachusetts Institute of Technology, recipient of a master's degree in management from the Sloan School of Management and a Harvard doctorate in organizational behaviour, Kotter was one of the youngest individuals to be given a full professorship at Harvard Business School in 1980, at the age of 33.

Kotter is a prolific and award-winning contributor to *Harvard Business Review* and is probably the world's most sought-after speaker on leadership and organizational change.

'Leadership produces change. That is its primary function.' That was the key statement in Kotter's influential book *A Force for Change* (1990), which defined the differences between leadership and management and the relationship between the two, based on rigorous casework within large US corporations. Since his first major book, *The General Managers* (1982), which analysed the capabilities and working methods of 15 general managers in a variety of companies, Kotter has always founded his research firmly on observation within organizations.

The General Managers, like Henry Mintzberg's *The Nature of Managerial Work*, exploded some long-held beliefs, principally the myth of the 'generalist' professional manager who could step into any business and run it. Instead, he discovered that the most effective GMs executed their work through a knowledge of the business and networks of other people in the organization, built up over a long period. He also illuminated the daunting complexity of the general manager's job and the dual competencies needed for handling both job responsibilities and developing relationships – skills in the latter role being particularly noticeable in the highest performers. Although nearly 20 years out of date in its research (executive mobility is much higher in the late 1990s), *The General Managers* remains a seminal work in its field.

In *A Force for Change*, Kotter applied a similar methodology of observation and identified the principal tasks of leadership as:

- Establishing direction, developing a vision and strategies for the future of the business
- Aligning people – getting others to 'understand, accept and line up in the chosen direction'
- Motivating and inspiring people by appealing to very basic but often untapped human needs, values and emotions

Management roles, on the other hand, were defined as:

- Planning and budgeting, setting short- to medium-term targets
- Establishing steps to reach them and allocating resources
- organising and staffing, establishing an organizational structure to accomplish the plan, staffing the jobs; communicating the plan, delegating responsibility and establishing systems to monitor implementation
- Controlling and problem-solving, monitoring results, identifying problems and organising to solve them

Both are 'complete action systems,' because leadership as

well as management involves implementation. Organizations need both strong management and strong leadership to succeed; strong management and weak leadership can produce stifling bureaucracy, whereas strong leadership without strong management can turn messianic and cult-like.

Direction-setting should not be confused with long-range planning, says Kotter. 'Planning is a managerial process that is not the same as, nor ever a substitute for, the direction-setting aspect of leadership, a process that produces vision and strategies, not plans . . . .'

Planning works as a complementary activity to direction-setting: 'a competent planning process serves as a useful reality check on direction-setting activities . . . Likewise, a competent direction-setting process provides a focus in which planning can then realistically be carried out; it clarifies what planning must be done and what planning is irrelevant.'

Similarly, Kotter argues, alignment is very different from the managerial process of organizing – it is 'a complicated communications challenge . . . Organizations that are both well led and well managed understand all this.'

The third task of leadership, motivation, is also very different from the incentives that managers employ in getting targets met. Management processes are about control and monitoring whereas leadership processes 'accomplish their energizing effect, not by pushing people in the right direction . . . but by satisfying very basic human needs: for achievement, belonging, recognition, self-esteem, a sense of control over one's life, and living up to one's ideals.'

Having examined these tasks in action in a number of closely observed companies, Kotter moves on to determine the inherent attributes commonly found in leaders. Such individuals, he concludes, always seem to have:

- Above-average energy levels
- An inner drive often associated with high personal standards, a certain dissatisfaction with the status quo, and a tendency to push for continuous improvement
- Above-average intellectual skills, e.g. in absorbing and processing large quantities of diverse information

- Mental or emotional health
- Integrity

Early broadening experience also helps: Kotter's research suggests that leaders in big jobs have almost always had an earlier opportunity to grow beyond the narrow base of most managerial careers.

A further message of the book is that effective leadership today is rarely the result of one person but of hundreds of individuals at middle levels in the organization. As early as 1984, Procter and Gamble's paper products division was pursuing a policy of group management in which the new divisional head invited his eleven direct reports to form a divisional 'board' and set strategy and direction. The result in 1986, after resources were diverted to a new product development, was the stunning rise of the Pampers brand of disposable nappies, from 40 per cent to 58 per cent of the market.

In *The Leadership Factor* (1987) Kotter had presented extensive evidence that the typical business organization did a poor job of finding people with leadership potential and developing it. Asserting that leadership is 'no longer the domain of the CEO or a few top managers, but is increasingly needed in nearly all managerial jobs,' he examined 15 US firms with high reputations for leadership development to identify the practices they followed, concluding among other things that a common factor was 'moderately strong corporate cultures.'

From here, after *A Force for Change*, it was a natural progression to *Corporate Culture and Performance* (1992), in which Kotter and co-author James L. Heskett demonstrated, again through a detailed study of successful turned-around companies, that cultures which encourage leadership up and down the hierarchy help organizations to adapt to change and thereby prosper. 'The single most visible factor that distinguishes major cultural changes that succeed from those that fail is competent leadership at the top. . . Unlike even the very best management process, leadership has as its primary function the production of change.'

Most companies, argued Kotter and Heskett, lack

adaptive cultures, and 'only with leadership does one get the boldness, the vision and the energy needed to create large and difficult changes . . .' Their ten case studies, including British Airways, General Electric, ICI and Nissan, all had a history of major cultural change – and subsequent enhanced performance – after an individual with a past track record of leadership was appointed at the top.

Leading Change (1996) pursued this theme by examining 100 cases of large-scale change, the book's title deliberately challenging the more common concept of 'managing change.' It identified eight best-practice stages in the process, all of them 'a leadership activity,' in which managers and executives:

- Help push up a sense of urgency
- Organise a guiding change coalition
- Create an appropriate change vision
- Communicate that vision to everyone
- Empower people to act on that vision
- Create short-term wins to build credibility
- Use that momentum to take on bigger change problems
- Institutionalise new approaches in the organizational culture

Kotter intends to develop his leadership studies further in future, believing that it is still growing in importance as a subject, and one about which we still know relatively little.

KEY WRITINGS

Kotter, J. P. (1982) 'What Effective General Managers Really Do' Cambridge, Mass.: *Harvard Business Review* (Nov/Dec).
Kotter, J. P. (1982) *The General Managers*, New York: Free Press.
Kotter, J. P. (1987) *The Leadership Factor*, New York: Free Press.

Kotter, J. P. (1990) 'What Leaders Really Do' Cambridge, Mass.: *Harvard Business Review* (May/June), reprint no. 90309.

Kotter, J. P (1990) *A Force for Change*, New York: Free Press.

Kotter, J. P. and Heskett, J. L. (1992) *Corporate Culture and Performance*, New York: Free Press.

Kotter, J. P. 'Leading Change: Why Transformation Efforts Fail', Cambridge, Mass.: *Harvard Business Review* (March/April), reprint no. 95204.

Kotter, J. P. (1996) *Leading Change*, Boston: Harvard Business School Press.

Kotter, J. P. (1997) *Matshusita Leadership*, Boston: Harvard Business School Press.

23

THEODORE LEVITT

(b. 1925)

Understanding the true role of marketing

The first management theorist to emphasize the importance of marketing, German-born Levitt, who has been associated with Harvard Business School for over 30 years, is unusual in having established his reputation as a guru on the basis of a single article – 'Marketing Myopia', published in the *Harvard Business Review* in the summer of 1960. It has since sold more than 500,000 reprinted copies.

In this extraordinarily influential article, Levitt argued powerfully that 'an industry is a customer-satisfying process, not a goods-producing process.' He suggested, for example, that railway managers helped to cause problems in their industry by viewing their business as railways, a technical product, rather than transport, a customer business. This was the approach reversed by Lord King and Sir Colin Marshall at British Airways, and which led to a dramatic turnround in the airline's performance and in the perception of it by its customers. Before Levitt, it has been said, marketing was a poor relation in the world of senior management. Levitt can claim to have had more articles published in the *Harvard Business Review* than any other guru. He edited the journal from 1986 to 1990, when he was succeeded by Rosabeth Moss Kanter. Of his five books on marketing, he regards *The Marketing Imagination* (1983) as his most important. He believes the secret of success in marketing is constantly to 'ask questions to develop your sensitivity and sensibility . . . perceptiveness reqquires cognitive effort and personal involvement. You bring something to what you see.'

Like other gurus, notably Kenichi Ohmae, Levitt has recently diversified into the subject of the global market-place and 'global branding.' Selling the same product worldwide, whether baked beans or cameras, is a subject of divided opinions among gurus; Ohmae, for example, taking the view that acting as an 'insider' in the territory you are selling in is more important than selling a stan-dard product from a central point, whereas Levitt inclines to the latter view.

Levitt's view of his own influence is modest. 'What I've achieved, I think, is to make myself effective in some way, kept myself intellectually curious, alive and produc-tive, and made myself interesting to myself' (*Makers of Management*: Clutterbuck and Crainer).

Theodore Levitt's ground-breaking article 'Marketing Myopia' started by pointing out that every industry was once a growth industry. After growth continues for a while, managers tend to believe it will always do so. Seeing no competition for their product, they pin their faith on improvements in productivity and cost reduction. The result is stagnation or decline.

Levitt proceeds to demonstrate that only 'a thoroughly customer-oriented management' can keep a growth industry growing 'even after the obvious opportunities have been exhausted'.

Detroit's automobile industry provided a key case study for Levitt's thesis. Ruled by the production ('Fordist') philosophy, it went on giving the customer what it believed the customer should have. 'Detroit never really researched the customer's wants,' wrote Levitt. 'It only researched the kinds of things which it had already decided to offer him.'

It was not until Japanese and European manufacturers

won huge sales with compact cars that Detroit woke up to the reality of a shift in its traditional customer base.

Other long-successful industries, Levitt suggested, could be overtaken by the same nemesis unless they reversed the habits of an organizational lifetime and realized that 'an industry begins with the customer and his needs, not with a patent, a raw material, or a selling skill.'

Selling, Levitt insisted, was not the same as marketing. 'Selling concerns itself with the tricks and techniques of getting people to exchange their cash for your product. It is not concerned with the values that the exchange is all about. And it does not, as marketing invariably does, view the entire business process as consisting of a tightly integrated effort to discover, create, arouse and satisfy customer needs.'

The difference between marketing and selling, Levitt continued, was 'more than semantic. Selling focuses on the needs of the seller, marketing on the needs of the buyer. Selling is preoccupied with the seller's need to convert his product into cash; marketing with the idea of satisfying the needs of the customer by means of the product and the whole cluster of things associated with creating, delivering and finally consuming it.'

In a truly marketing-oriented firm, says Levitt, what is offered for sale is much more than the basic product or service – how it is made available to the customer, for example, under what conditions and terms of trade. 'Most important, what it offers for sale is determined not by the seller but by the buyer . . . the product becomes a consequence of the marketing effort, not vice versa.'

Taking a deliberately bizarre example of an industry that could have prevented its demise by understanding the wants of its customers, Levitt cites the makers of buggy whips in the early days of the automobile. 'No amount of product improvement could stave off its death sentence. But had the industry defined itself as being in the transportation business rather than the buggy whip business, it might have survived. It would have done what survival always entails, that is, changing. Even if it had only defined its business as providing a stimulant or catalyst to an energy source, it might have survived by becoming a manufacturer of, say, fanbelts or air cleaners.'

In *The Marketing Imagination*, Levitt argued that competitive success rested on realizing five factors:

1. The purpose of a business is to create and keep customers.
2. To do this, goods and services must be produced and delivered that people want and value, at prices and conditions that are more attractive than those of competitors.
3. To continue, enough profits must be made to keep investors.
4. To achieve this, all companies must clarify their purposes, strategies and plans, and clearly communicate them to the workforce. The larger the enterprise, the greater the need for a clearly written and reviewed set of goals.
5. All enterprises must have a system of rewards, audits and controls to ensure the proper pursuit of those goals.

The organization, Levitt constantly preaches, must think of itself less in terms of producing goods or services and more in terms of buying customers. To achieve this, the chief executive's leadership is all-important.

Today marketing is no longer, as Levitt called it in 1960, a 'stepchild.' Getting and staying close to the customer was enshrined by Tom Peters and Robert Waterman's *In Search of Excellence* as a prime component of the top-performing company. But that was in 1982. More than 20 years earlier, the idea was sufficiently novel for Levitt's *Harvard Business Review* article to start an earthquake in management thinking.

KEY WRITINGS

Levitt, T. (1960) 'Marketing Myopia', Cambridge, Mass.: *Harvard Business Review*.

Levitt, T. (1962) *Innovation in Marketing*, New York: McGraw-Hill.

Levitt, T. (1969) *The Marketing Mode*, New York: McGraw-Hill.

Levitt, T. (1983) *The Marketing Imagination*, New York: Free Press.

RENSIS LIKERT

(1903–1981)

*How leadership styles link with business
performance*

US social psychologist and researcher who founded in
1949 a pioneering establishment for research into human
behaviour in organizations, the Institute for Social
Research at the University of Michigan. His work had a
lasting effect on organizational theory and the study of
leadership. He is best known for his *New Patterns of
Management* (1961), in which, based on extensive questioning of employees in industrial firms, he argued that
the management of organizations could be categorized
along a line graduating from System 1, exploitative and
authoritarian, to System 4, participative and based on
overlapping work groups. He also invented the concept
of 'linking plans' – individuals capable of linking each
work group to the organization.

Like Douglas McGregor (qv), Likert rejected traditional
assumptions about human behaviour under management
and proposed new methods based on a better understanding of people's motivation and potential.

Likert gained a Ph.D. from Columbia University in
1932, and his work there was later published as 'A
Technique for the Measurement of Attitudes.' He then
became director of research at a life insurance office in
Hartford, Connecticut, where he began to study management practices. In 1939 he moved to the Department of
Agriculture in Washington as director of program surveys.

From 1949 to 1969 he ran the Institute for Social Research and on retirement formed his own consulting firm. His books are underpinned with numerous original research studies, the last of them being written with his wife and co-researcher, Jane Gibson Likert.

Rensis Likert believed that participative management was the best kind, and the most likely to produce results. Some of his contemporary management thinkers criticized him for flatly assuming that group discussion was the only way to good decision-making and thereby abandoning or ignoring the search for better techniques of problem-solving or decision-making.

Kepner and Tregoe in *The Rational Manager* (1965) commented that managers would find this both difficult and 'far removed from the practical reality they must contend with every day.'

Likert's primary objective at the Institute for Social Research was to identify different styles of leadership and correlate them with business performance. His research method was based on detailed questionnaires to employees of US companies, asking them a series of questions about their supervisors. He then drew up a profile of each supervisor or manager in the light of how he was viewed by the people who worked under him. From these profiles Likert established his System 1 to 4 progressive chart of management styles:

1. Exploitative authoritarian: management by fear and coercion, where communication is top-down, decision-making is done at the top with no shared processes, and superiors and subordinates are psychologically far apart.
2. Benevolent authoritarian: management by carrot rather than stick, but subordinates are still basically subservient; such information as flows upwards is mainly what the boss is thought to want to hear, and policy decisions are taken at the top, with only minor ones delegated to a

lower level.

3. Consultative: management uses both carrot and stick and does try to talk to employees; communication flows both ways but is still somewhat limited upwards; important decisions are still taken top-down.

4. Participative: management provides economic rewards and is concerned to get employees involved in groups capable of making decisions; it sets challenging goals and works closely with employees to encourage high performance. Communication flows easily in both directions and sideways to peers; superiors and subordinates are psychologically close. Decision-making is done through participative processes: work groups are integrated into the formal structure of the organization by creating a series of overlapping groups with each linked to the rest of the organization by a 'linking pin' – preferably a team leader or departmental manager, who will be a member of both group and management.

Likert's research suggested that departments which were low in efficiency tended to be in the charge of 'job-centred' supervisors; that is, Taylorist managers who keep their subordinates busily engaged in a 'specified work cycle in a prescribed way and at a satisfactory rate as determined by time standards.'

Supervisors with the best record of performance tended to be 'employee-centred,' to regard their chief task as dealing with people rather than work and who focused on building effective work groups that in turn were set high achievement goals. Such supervisors exercised general rather than detailed supervision of their subordinates and were more concerned with overall targets than with methods. They also allowed the maximum participation in decision-making.

In *New Ways of Managing Conflict*, Likert and his wife profile the System 4 Total Model Organization (System 4T), which adds certain characteristics to System 4, such as high levels of performance goals, transmitted by leader to subordinates; a high level of skill and knowledge on the part of the leader, and the leader's capacity to provide planning, resources, equipment and help for subordinates. System 4T is the optimum Likert structure in terms of linkages and group working relationships, and he conceives it as the best means of dealing with conflict in an organization.

Likert argues that the nearer an organization approaches to System 4T, the more its productivity and profitability will improve and conflict be reduced. Beyond this, he also suggests a System 5 for the future, in which all authority on a hierarchy basis will disappear, such authority as individuals retain deriving only from their 'linking pin' roles and the overlapping of groups.

The basic principle behind the work of both Likert and McGregor is that effective modern organizations must see themselves as interacting groups of people with supporting relationships to each other. The ideal goal is to achieve an organization in which the organization's objectives become of personal significance to everyone working in it. In pursuit of this, management must be a relative process, always adapting itself to the individual human beings who are led by it.

KEY WRITINGS

Likert, R. (1961) *New Patterns of Management*, New York: McGraw-Hill.

Likert, R. (1967) *The Human Organization: Its Management and Value*, New York: McGraw-Hill.

Likert, R. and Likert, J. G. (1976) *New Ways of Managing Conflict*, New York: McGraw-Hill.

DOUGLAS McGREGOR

(1906–1964)

Theory X and Theory Y: authoritarian vs participative management

US social psychologist specializing in human behaviour within organizations, and famous for his formulation of 'Theory X' (authoritarian management) and 'Theory Y' (participative management), first propounded in his 1960 book *The Human Side of Enterprise*.

For some years president of Antioch College, McGregor was professor of management at the Massachusetts Institute of Technology from 1954 until his death in 1964.

McGregor shared many of his ideas on human wants with Abraham Maslow (qv) and Rensis Likert (qv). Maslow experimented with Theory Y in a California electronics plant and concluded that it did not wholly work in practice. Further work on motivating human achievement which revealed Theory Y as insufficiently flexible was done after McGregor's death by David C. McClelland of Harvard.

However, in 1994 Robert H. Waterman Jr. revealed in *Frontiers of Excellence* that in 1956 McGregor was invited by an executive of Procter and Gamble, David Swanson, who had been a student of McGregor's at MIT, to design a detergent plant in Augusta, Georgia, on Theory Y principles. Swanson had served with the US army in Korea and returned to civilian life convinced that military command-and-control structures were totally unsuitable for a business organization, which should be drawing out responsibility and potential in the individual.

The Augusta plant, designed for a non-hierarchical organization working in self-managed teams, was an immediate success. By the mid-1960s it was 30 per cent more productive than any other P&G plant. The company spread the principle through other plants and kept the story secret for 40 years, regarding it as a competitive advantage.

Since the mid-1990s, self-managed teams have become an accepted part of organizational change and empowerment. McGregor's legacy as a teacher and thinker influenced a whole generation of management theorists, including Charles Handy and Warren Bennis (qv). It has made him one of the most powerful, if under-recognized, gurus of the century.

Douglas McGregor believed that the way an organization was run stemmed directly from the beliefs of its managers. 'Behind every managerial decision or action are assumptions about human nature and human behaviour,' he wrote in *The Human Side of Enterprise*, probably the most widely read and quoted of all the books on motivation in industry published since World War II.

The research behind Theory X and Theory Y was not original but, as McGregor acknowledged, it synthesized and formulated from the ideas of others (including, as Peter Drucker has observed, those Drucker himself had presented in three early books: *Concept of the Corporation*, *The New Society* and *The Practice of Management*).

McGregor had already suggested the term Theory X to define a set of assumptions that had ruled management thinking since the writings of Henri Fayol. Theory X assumes that most people are lazy, dislike work and need a mixture of carrot and stick to perform; that they are basically immature, need direction and are incapable of taking responsibility. Theory Y assumes the opposite; that people actually have a psychological need to work and want achievement and responsibility – that they are adult, in fact. On this reading, Periclean Athens was a Theory Y society, Sparta a Theory X society.

McGregor believed that Theory X owed its origins to the banishment of Adam and Eve from Eden into a world where they were forced to work to survive. 'The stress that management places on productivity, on the concept of "a fair day's work," on the evils of featherbedding and restriction of output, on rewards for performance – while it has a logic in terms of the objectives of enterprise – reflects an underlying belief that management must counteract an inherent human tendency to avoid work.'

Like Maslow with his hierarchy of needs, McGregor identified a series of human wants in ascending order, from the most basic physiological urges through a desire for safety and security (and security in the workplace) to the 'social needs' such as belonging, acceptance by one's peers and the giving and receiving of affection. Above those again came the 'egoistic needs' – those that relate to an individual's self-esteem, his need for self-respect, self-confidence, autonomy, achievement, competence and knowledge; and to reputation, status, recognition and the respect of one's peers. Ultimately in McGregor's pyramid came the needs for self-fulfilment, for realizing one's individual potential and for continuing in self-development.

'Man is a wanting animal – as soon as one of his needs is satisfied, another appears in its place,' wrote McGregor in *The Human Side of Enterprise*. 'This process is unending. It continues from birth to death. Man continuously puts forth effort . . . to satisfy his needs.'

Since most modern managements by McGregor's time were providing relatively well for both physiological and safety needs, the motivational emphasis had shifted to social, egoistic and self-fulfilment needs. 'Unless there are opportunities at work to satisfy these higher-level needs, people will be deprived; and their behaviour will reflect this deprivation,' wrote McGregor.

If management continued to focus its attention on physiological needs, therefore, providing rewards was unlikely to

133

be effective, and the only alternative under this philosophy would be reliance on the threat of punishment. Thus part of Theory X validates itself, 'but only because we have mistaken effects for causes.'

McGregor continues: 'The philosophy of management by direction and control – regardless of whether it is hard or soft – is inadequate to motivate because the human needs on which this approach relies are relatively unimportant motivators of behaviour in our society today. Direction and control are of limited value in motivating people whose important needs are social and egoistic . . . So long as the assumptions of Theory X continue to influence managerial strategy, we will fail to discover, let alone utilize, the potentialities of the average human being.'

Theory Y, the management approach designed to tap these potentialities, was based on McGregor's observations of the way management thinking had moved a considerable way from the traditional 'hard' approach and the 'soft' reaction that followed the Depression years. He formulated six basic assumptions for Theory Y:

1. 'The expenditure of physical and mental effort on work is as natural as play or rest. The average human being does not inherently dislike work. Depending upon controllable conditions, work may be a source of satisfaction (and will be voluntarily performed) or a source of punishment (and will be avoided if possible).
2. 'External control and the threat of punishment are not the only means for bringing about effort towards organizational objectives. Man will exercise self-direction and self-control in the service of objectives to which he is committed.
3. 'Commitment to objectives is a function of the rewards associated with their achievement. The most significant of such rewards, e.g. the satisfaction of ego and self-actualisation needs, can be direct products of effort directed towards organizational objectives.
4. 'The average human being learns, under proper conditions, not only to accept but to seek responsibility.
5. 'The capacity to exercise a relatively high degree of

imagination, ingenuity and creativity in the solution of organizational problems is widely, not narrowly, distributed in the population.

6. 'Under the conditions of modern industrial life, the intellectual potentialities of the average human being are only partially utilized.'

Such assumptions, McGregor pointed out, had a deep implication for management. Where Theory X offered management an easy scapegoat for failure – the innate nature and limitations of its human resources – Theory Y placed all problems 'squarely in the lap of management.' If employees were lazy or unwilling to show initiative or responsibility, if they were indifferent or intransigent, the fault lay in management methods. In other words, McGregor was redefining the old military adage: 'There are no bad troops, only bad officers.'

McGregor admitted that Theory Y was not perfect and remained to be tested in a variety of organizations. His disciple Abraham Maslow (qv) found it to be wanting in a well-meaning experiment run on its principles in a California electronics factory. Maslow believed it placed too much of a burden on individuals who actually wanted guidance, direction and some form of authority.

Peter Drucker has commented: 'It has now become clear that Theory X and Theory Y are not, as McGregor maintained, theories about human nature . . . Ordinary, everyday experience teaches us that the same people react quite differently to different circumstances. They may be lazy and resist work to the point of sabotaging it in one situation. They may be motivated to achievement in another one. It is clearly not human nature nor personality structure that is at issue.'

Drucker also referred to the work of David C. McClelland of Harvard, especially his book *Motivating Economic Achievement* (Free Press, 1969), who concluded that the desire to achieve is conditioned largely by culture and experience, both of which can be changed.

McGregor never claimed that Theory Y denied all need for authority, only that it denied that authority was

135

appropriate for all purposes, including the goal of 'obtaining commitment to objectives.'

'Theory Y assumes that people will exercise self-direction and self-control in the achievement of organizational objectives to the degree that they are committed to those objectives . . . Managerial policies and practices materially affect this degree of commitment.'

Put simply, McGregor believed that human beings were capable of far greater potential than the industrial management of his time could understand. Theory X denied even the existence of that potential: Theory Y challenged management 'to innovate, to discover new ways of organizing and directing human effort, even though we recognize that the perfect organization, like the perfect vacuum, is practically out of reach.'

History, starting with the Procter and Gamble plant in Augusta, Georgia, continues to vindicate the essential rightness and power of his thinking.

(All quotations from McGregor are from *The Human Side of Enterprise*, reproduced in *Organization Theory*, ed. D. S. Pugh (Penguin 1990).)

KEY WRITINGS

McGregor, D. (1960) *The Human Side of Enterprise*, New York: McGraw-Hill.
McGregor, D. (1966) *Leadership and Motivation*, MIT Press.
McGregor, D. (1967) *The Professional Manager*, New York: McGraw-Hill.

26

ABRAHAM MASLOW

(1908-1970)

The 'hierarchy of needs' in motivation

New York-born psychologist and behavioural scientist whom Peter Drucker dubbed 'the father of humanist psychology.' Maslow invented the term 'hierarchy of needs' to account for the roots of human motivation.

He trained at the University of Wisconsin and broke an academic career between 1947 and 1949 to work in industry, returning to teaching at Brandeis University, Massachusetts, where he became a professor and head of department. He then spent some further time in industry, studying Douglas McGregor's Theory Y in action at a California electronics factory, where he concluded that McGregor's theory, which he had much admired, did not work in reality because it ignored the need for the structure and certainties provided by the authoritarian Theory X.

Maslow's essential optimism about the good qualities of human nature was part of its time in the climate of the postwar years, and his ideas were influential on other behavioural scientists such as Chris Argyris (qv), McGregor himself (qv), Rensis Likert (qv) and Frederick Herzberg (qv).

Maslow's 'hierarchy of needs' postulated that once an individual's basic physiological needs had been satisfied – and these included not only warmth, food and sexual fulfilment, but also a safe, structured environment – the higher needs of love, esteem and fulfilment of personal potential would be released. His greatest insight was to realize that none of these wants is absolute; as soon as one is satisfied, the fact of its satisfaction ceases to be important.

'But what Maslow did not see,' observes Drucker in his classic *Management: Tasks, Responsibilities, Practices*,

> is that a want changes in the act of being satisfied. As the economic want becomes satisfied, that is, as people no longer have to subordinate every other human need and human value to getting the next meal, it becomes less and less satisfying to obtain more economic rewards. This does not mean that the economic rewards become less important. On the contrary, while the ability of the economic reward to provide a positive incentive diminishes, its capacity to create dissatisfaction, if disappointed, rapidly increases. In Herzberg's words, economic rewards cease to be 'incentives' and become 'hygiene factors.' If not properly taken care of – that is, if there is dissatisfaction with the economic rewards – they become deterrents.
>
> This we now know to be true of every one of Maslow's wants. As a want approaches satiety, its capacity to reward, and with it its power as an incentive, diminishes fast. But its capacity to deter, to create dissatisfaction, and to act as a disincentive, rapidly increases.

Drucker pointed out that, once a need was satisfied, ever-greater incentives were needed to maintain the same level of satisfaction, and that in the economic sphere, the danger was that additional rewards would become progressively viewed as rights or entitlements.

Maslow's experience in the California electronics company proved valuable in applying practical research to Douglas McGregor's highly theoretical proposition ('Theory Y') that most people want to work, achieve and take responsibility; in short, that most people are naturally adult, as opposed to the 'Theory X' view of humans as basically immature and in need of direction.

Maslow's discovery – in a company which believed wholeheartedly in Theory Y – was that even an organization composed of strong and mature individuals needs the security of some structure and some direction. He criticized McGregor, his mentor, for 'inhumanity' to the weak, the vulnerable and the immature, who could not take the burden of individual responsibility. Nevertheless, he remained a convinced advocate of the underlying soundness of Theory Y and his solution was that Theory X could and should be replaced by an improved version of Theory Y. This would be more demanding in many ways than the authoritarian prescription, because it required more of individuals.

By extension, as Drucker points out, this argument applies with even more force to flexible, free-form organizations, because these place a greater load on their members than do the traditional, control-and-command structures.

KEY WRITING

Maslow, A. H. (1970) *Motivation and Personality*, New York: Harper and Row.

ELTON W. MAYO

(1880–1949)

Human relations in industry and respect for individuals

Australian-born Mayo is regarded as the founder of industrial sociology, particularly the 'Human Relations Movement,' based on his discoveries in the Hawthorne Experiments of 1927-32 of what really motivates workers to higher performance.

A graduate of Adelaide University and a medical student in London and Edinburgh, Mayo taught mental and moral philosophy at the University of Queensland between 1911 and 1919. In 1923 he emigrated to the United States, where he worked first on a three-year research project at a Pennsylvania textile mill, prior to joining Harvard University as associate professor of industrial research in 1926.

Mayo spent most of his career at Harvard, ending up as professor of industrial research in the Graduate School of Business Administration. He was also a consultant on industrial problems to the postwar British Labour government led by Clement Attlee.

Elton Mayo's most important finding was to identify the roots of work satisfaction as non-economic and to connect them more with the interest taken in a worker's performance than with financial reward. In this, he reversed the emphasis on the incentive of monetary reward which had been the conventional wisdom ever since the writings of F. W. Taylor. Workers rejected 'Taylorism,' Mayo explained, because in spite of its aids to efficiency it was basically an imposed system, not one that took account of the employees' own views.

The vital importance of management–worker communication, a key Mayo discovery, laid the foundation for the work of many later management thinkers and writers, including Peters and Waterman (*In Search of Excellence*) and the 1950s school of sociologists headed by Chris Argyris, Frederick Herzberg and Abraham Maslow.

The Hawthorne Experiments with which Mayo's name is forever linked were named after Western Electric's Hawthorne Works in Chicago. They ran from 1927 to 1932 under Mayo's leadership (and a further five years after that), and were conducted by a team of Harvard scientists and between 75 and 100 investigators working with 20,000 Western Electric employees.

The experiments arose from an earlier series of tests by Western Electric which had involved changes in working conditions and produced unexpected results in employee performance. Two teams of workers took part in these tests, in which the lighting conditions for one group only were improved. Production in that group rose dramatically – but so it did in the group for which the lighting remained unchanged.

Mayo took this further, making as many as ten changes in working conditions such as shorter hours, varied rest-breaks and a number of incentives. Mayo's research team spent a great deal of time with the work groups – each consisting of six women – discussing the changes before they were put into effect. Output increased each time a change was made. Yet when the teams were asked to return to their original working conditions, with a 48-hour week, no incentives and no rest breaks, output rose again – indeed, to the highest ever recorded at Hawthorne. Other significant results included a decline in absenteeism of 80 per cent.

The only explanation, Mayo concluded in one of his

later works, was that the employees had gained enormously in work satisfaction by the feeling that they were teams of individuals, not cogs in a machine, and by the communication between researchers and workers, leading to everyone feeling more valued and responsible for her performance and that of the group as a whole. This sense of cohesiveness and self-esteem was more important to performance than any number of improvements in the working environment.

Although Mayo did not crystallize his findings until years after the Hawthorne Experiments, a contemporary series of interviews in the Chicago works established an equally important discovery: that worker-management conflict may often be due less to the ostensible reasons for a dispute, such as tea-breaks or insufficient light, than to basic emotional attitudes. Workers were ruled by the 'logic of sentiment,' thought Mayo, whereas managers were activated by the 'logic of cost and efficiency.' Thus, without understanding and compromise, conflict was inevitable.

The ultimate importance of the Hawthorne experiments was their demonstration, in Mayo's view, that the dour Taylorist philosophy of self-interest was disproved: that workers valued spontaneous cooperation and creative relationships among those with whom they worked, and would perform accordingly. 'The desire to stand well with one's fellows, the so-called human instinct of association, easily outweighs the merely individual interest and the logic of reasoning upon which so many spurious principles of management are based,' wrote Mayo in *The Social Problems of an Industrial Civilization*.

Mayo was not, however, against scientific management, for all that he debunked Taylor's rigid application of it. 'Observation – skill – experiment and logic – these must be regarded as the three stages of advancement,' he observed in the same book. Mayo believed that his findings disproved what he called the 'rabble hypothesis' of society as 'a horde of unorganized individuals,' each of whom 'acts in a manner calculated to secure his self-preservation or self-interest.'

Two later sociological writers, D. C. Miller and W. H. Form, developed eight principal conclusions from Mayo's researches in their book *Industrial Sociology*, quoted in J. A. C. Brown's *The Social Psychology of Industry* (1954):

1 Work is a group activity.
2 The social world of the adult is primarily patterned about work activity.
3 The need for recognition, security, and sense of belonging is more important in determining a worker's morale and productivity than the physical conditions under which he works.
4 A complaint is not necessarily an objective recital of facts; it is commonly a symptom manifesting disturbance of an individual's status position.
5 The worker is a person whose attitudes and effectiveness are conditioned by social demands from both inside and outside the work plant.
6 Informal groups within the work plant exercise strong social controls over the work habits and attitudes of the individual worker.
7 The change from an established to an adaptive society . . . tends continually to disrupt the social organization of a work plant and industry generally.
8 Group collaboration does not occur by accident; it must be planned for and developed. If group collaboration is achieved, the work relations within a work plant may reach a cohesion which resists the disrupting effects of adaptive society.

Another writer on industrial psychology in the 1950s, Gordon Rattray Taylor, estimated from his observations of firms which had put similar principles into practice that by using such methods Britain could expand its national income by 50 per cent within five years without additional capital investment, and that the price of many manufactured goods could be reduced by a third. Needless to say, the experiment has never been carried out on a sufficiently wide scale to prove or disprove his theory.

Mayo's discovery of the importance of the peer group at work led him to conclude that within each formal organization existed many informal ones which could be encouraged to greater productivity by being led to do it themselves, through interest and respect on the part of their managers.

More profoundly, Mayo believed that by creating such an atmosphere of spontaneous cooperation in industry, society at large could help to combat the postwar collapse in traditional values. This, for him, remained one of the most important tasks facing a manager. The whole Human Relations movement, as engendered by Mayo's work, became concerned with discovering, through scientific research, how to harness the motivation and commitment of individuals to corporate goals.

Mayo's contribution to management thinking was seminal. It revealed the importance, in hard bottom-line terms, of human emotions, reactions and respect to the business of managing others. It also pioneered the whole concept of proper management-worker communication – again a new idea because of the respect for the individual it required between bosses and workers.

Management, Mayo demonstrated once and for all, could only succeed in leading an organization's employees if the workers, in their informal groups, accepted that leadership without reservation. In his own words, Mayo identified the importance of the Hawthorne findings as specifying, quite clearly, that the relation of working groups to management was one of the fundamental problems of large-scale industry. Organizing teamwork – developing and sustaining cooperation – had to be a major preoccupation of management. Above all, management needed to think less about what 'we' wanted to get across to 'them' than to listen to what 'they' wanted to know and would be receptive to.

'The human relations prescription, though rarely practised, remains the classic formula,' wrote Peter Drucker in 1973. It is still too rarely practised, though every management pays lip service to it.

ELTON W. MAYO

KEY WRITINGS

Mayo, E. (1933) *The Human Problems of an Industrial Civilisation*, London: Macmillan.
Mayo, E. (1949) *The Social Problems of an Industrial Civilisation*, London: Routledge and Kegan Paul.

HENRY MINTZBERG

(b. 1939)

How strategy is made and how managers use their time

Canadian-born professor of management at McGill University, Montreal, and at INSEAD, the international business school at Fontainebleau, France. His immensely influential work falls into three main categories: strategy-making; what managers actually do with their time (as opposed to what they think they do), and how their mental processes work (the 'right brain, left brain' theories); and how organizations design themselves to suit their needs.

Mintzberg, originally an engineering graduate of McGill who later studied at the Sloan School of Management, Massachusetts Institute of Technology, is one of the most accessible of management writers, with an easy style and refreshingly iconoclastic approach. He has written over 100 monographs and articles as well as nine books. His reputation is high among those who study the arts of strategic management and planning, about which he wrote a typically provocative history in 1994 entitled *The Rise and Fall of Strategic Planning*.

His teaching work is more international and multicultural than that of any other leading guru. He is currently supervising a co-operative venture by five business schools in Canada, England, Japan, France and India which aims to create a next-generation programme of management education for practising managers in the context of their own jobs and the needs of their organizations. Mintzberg's view of conventional MBA courses is that they have minimal value in the real world of business: he likes to observe that 'You can't create a manager in the classroom.'

Mintzberg's reputation was made by *The Nature of Managerial Work*, published in 1973, and the article in *Harvard Business Review* in 1975 which brought it to a wider public ('The Manager's Job: Folklore and Fact'). In researching the book, he spent a week in each of five middle- to large-sized organizations – a consulting firm, a technology company, a hospital, a consumer goods company and a school system – observing how chief executive officers used their time, as well as reporting other studies of managers lower down the line, ranging from factory supervisors to hospital administrators.

Far from confirming any grand all-embracing role, such as Peter Drucker proposed in his analogy of the manager as orchestra conductor, Mintzberg found that a manager's time is constantly being fragmented by interruptions, but that these appeared to produce an adrenalin of their own and to convince the manager that he was achieving a great deal through responding to the pressures of the job over a great many issues, even in summary and incomplete fashion.

'Jumping from topic to topic, he (the manager) thrives on interruptions and, more often than not, disposes of items in ten minutes or less. Though he may have fifty projects going, all are delegated. He juggles them, checking each one periodically before sending it back into orbit.'

The four definitions of managerial work laid down by Henri Fayol in 1916 – planning, organization, coordination and control – have very little bearing on actual daily routine, Mintzberg discovered. Yet, as he explained in a *Harvard Business Review* article condensing the essence of his 1973 book, 'Without a proper answer, how can we teach management? How can we design planning or information systems for managers? How can we improve the practice of management at all?'

Half the activities engaged in by Mintzberg's five CEOs lasted less than nine minutes and only ten per cent exceeded one hour in duration. 'The chief executives met a steady stream of callers and mail from the moment they arrived in the morning until they left in the evening . . . A diary study of 160 British top and middle managers found that they worked for half an hour or more without interruption about once every two days.'

'The traditional literature notwithstanding, the job of managing does not breed reflective planners; the manager responds to stimuli as an individual who is conditioned by his job to prefer live to delayed action.'

The manager also spends as much time dealing with people outside as inside the company, Mintzberg found. 'He shuns written reports, skims periodicals and merely processes his mail.' He prefers to pick up his information verbally, at meetings and on the telephone, and indeed relies heavily on gossip and hearsay, inside and outside the company, to keep him up to date.

Indeed, Mintzberg concluded in a memorable finding, 'the executives I was studying – all very competent by any standard – were fundamentally indistinguishable from their counterparts of 100 years ago (or 1,000 years ago, for that matter). The information they need differs, but they seek it in the same way; by word of mouth. Their decisions concern modern technology, but the procedures they use are still the same as the procedures of the nineteenth-century manager.'

'Managers seem to cherish "soft" information, especially gossip, hearsay and speculation. Why? The reason is its timeliness: today's gossip may be tomorrow's fact. The manager who is not accessible for the telephone call informing him that his biggest customer was seen golfing with his main competitor may read about a dramatic drop in the next quarterly report. But by then it's too late.'

Furthermore, 'managers apparently do not write down much of what they hear. Thus the strategic data-bank of the organization is not in the memory of its computers but in the minds of its managers.'

Out of all this mass of material, which baldly contradicted most conventional wisdom about a manager's activities, Mintzberg identified ten principal managerial roles, grouped into three main areas – interpersonal, informational and decisional.

Interpersonal roles, in his definition, comprise three functions essential to a manager: those of figurehead, leader, and liaison. The first two are self-explanatory (the figurehead performs ceremonial roles such as making presentation speeches, meeting visiting dignitaries and lunching important clients; the leader hires, trains and motivates employees) while the third covers a manager's network of relationships within and without the organization, outside his vertical chain of command, and mainly in pursuit of building up a private information system. 'Managers spend as much time with peers and other people outside their units as they do with their own subordinates, and surprisingly little time with their own superiors.'

Informational roles involve those of monitor (keeping tabs on what's going on); disseminator (transmitting essential information to subordinates) and spokesman (the public voice of the unit). 'The manager emerges as the nerve centre of his organizational unit. He may not know everything, but he typically knows more than any member of his staff . . . Many of these contacts are with other managers of equal status, who are themselves nerve centres in their own organization. In this way the manager develops a powerful data base of information. The processing of information is a key part of the manager's job . . . In large part, communication is his work.'

Decisional roles, not surprisingly, are described as the most important. Mintzberg divides this category into four – entrepreneur, disturbance handler, resource allocator and negotiator.

As entrepreneur, the manager 'seeks to improve his unit and to adapt it to changing conditions' sometimes juggling as many as fifty different projects at a time, such as initiating a PR campaign, dealing with a poor cash-flow position, reorganizing a weak department or looking after the various stages of an acquisition. As disturbance handler, the manager reacts to events and change beyond his foresight or control; a strike, the bankruptcy of a major customer or the failure of a key supplier.

It is here that Mintzberg parts company most strikingly with Drucker's comparison of the manager's role to that of an orchestral conductor. 'In effect, every manager must spend a good part of his time responding to high-pressure disturbances.'

As resource allocator, the manager must decide how best to deploy the assets of the organization, including its human assets and, most importantly, the manager's own time. As negotiator, he is responsible for all the variety of decisions involved in dealing with other individuals; whether these concern a difficult sales contract, the threat of a strike, staff grievances or attracting a new star player to the team.

All the variables contained within these permutations led Mintzberg to conclude that management is an art rather than a teachable science, and that it requires a continuous process of self-education and assessment. He also pointed out that the roles are part of an integrated whole and cannot easily be separated when, for example, efforts are made to split a managerial job into internal and external roles, though not all managers, he found, give equal attention to all roles. (Sales managers tend to emphasize the interpersonal side, production managers the decisional roles and staff managers the informational roles.)

In summarizing the theme of his findings for the *Harvard Business Review* in 1975, Mintzberg said the pressures of his job 'drive the manager to be superficial in his actions – to overload himself with work, encourage interruption, respond quickly to every stimulus, seek the tangible and avoid the abstract, make decisions in small increments and do everything abruptly . . . the danger in managerial work is that (managers) will respond to every issue equally (and that means abruptly) and that they will never work the tangible bits and pieces of informational input into a comprehensive picture of their work.'

Management schools, he concluded, would only begin 'the serious training of managers when skill training takes a serious place next to cognitive learning. . . . Cognitive learning no more makes a manager than it does a swimmer. The latter will drown the first time he jumps into the water if his coach never takes him out of the lecture hall, gets him wet and gives him feedback on his performance.'

Managerial skills such as developing peer relationships, resolving conflicts, handling information and negotiations need to be practised, and the manager should be introspective enough about his work to go on learning on the job.

'No job is more vital to our society than that of the manager,' declared Mintzberg. 'It is the manager who determines whether our institutions serve us well or whether they squander our talents and resources. it is time to strip away the folklore about managerial work, and time to study it realistically so that we can begin the difficult task of making significant improvements in its performance.'

From analysing the components of managerial work, Mintzberg moved on to study the design of organizations in *The Structuring of Organizations* (1979) and *Structures in Fives: Designing Effective Organizations* (1983).

He concluded that most organizational structures fall into five basic categories: simple structure, machine bureaucracy, professional bureaucracy, divisionalized form and adhocracy – a term recently appropriated and redefined by Robert Waterman to describe the ideal conditions for a flexible, innovation-inducing organizational structure. (Waterman, author of *The Renewal Factor* and co-author with Tom Peters of the massively selling *In Search of Excellence*, acknowledges Mintzberg as one of his own most influential gurus.)

Mintzberg's simple structure organization is just that: a centralized, perhaps autocratic arrangement typical of the entrepreneur-founded company. There will be only a small hierarchy, and control is exercised by a strong chief executive. It is the sort of organization that attracts strong loyalty because of its simplicity, flexibility, informality and 'sense of mission' – but it is desperately vulnerable to the accidents of fate: 'one heart attack can literally wipe out the organization's prime co-ordinating mechanism.'

The machine bureaucracy, by contrast, gains its strength from what Mintzberg calls its 'technostructure' – its financial controllers, strategic planners, production experts. It is best at mass-production tasks and is characterized by many layers of management and formal procedures. It tends to be slow on its feet when reacting to change, and poor at motivating its employees. A large car assembly plant would be a typical example.

The professional bureaucracy is built less on hierarchy than on shared expertise – it might be a professional practice of some kind, a school or a hospital. Its administration is governed by standards set by independent professional bodies. It will tend to be more democratic and more highly motivated – among the professionals, if not their support workers – than the machine bureaucracy, but with its lines of authority less clearly set out.

The divisionalized form is reflected in the typical large multinational or industrial corporation where a small central core controls key guidelines for a number of otherwise autonomous units. Essentially, Mintzberg sees this as an off-shoot of the machine bureaucracy – several machine bureaucracies, in fact, operating under a central staff. It may have started life as a single machine bureaucracy which hived off into divisions as a result of geographic market diversifications.

The adhocracy is most often found in the new technology industries, which need constantly to innovate and respond quickly to changing markets. It is characterized by flexible, cross-border teams collaborating on specific projects as required, and of Mintzberg's five categories of organization 'shows the least reverence for the classical principles of management.'

Mintzberg's adhocracy has two sub-sections; the operating adhocracy, a creative unit working in the competitive marketplace, such as an advertising agency or software development company, and the administrative adhocracy, which may be research-based, like NASA.

Within Mintzberg's five basic organizational structures are five common elements: the 'strategic apex' of top executives (strongest in the simple structure); the 'technostructure' of key individuals in finance, training, personnel, planning and productin (strongest in the machine bureaucracy); the 'operating core' of those at the coalface of the organization (nurses and teachers in a professional bureaucracy, buyers and sales staff in a manufacturing machine bureaucracy); the 'middle line' of managers who link the strategic apex with the operating core (strongest in the divisionalized form); and finally, the 'support staff', who work in areas such as R&D, salaries, public relations and so on. In a manufacturing company their role, though important, is not the fulcrum that it is in the adhocracy, which relies on the quality of its R&D.

'If Simple Structure and Machine Bureaucracy were yesterday's structures, and Professional Bureaucracy and the Divisionalised Form are today's, then Adhocracy is clearly tomorrow's,' writes Mintzberg. But he does not rule out further evolutions of structure as different influences exert their pull, and he has identified one for the future, where ideological influences are involved, which he calls the Missionary. Examples include the Israeli kibbutz and the Japanese manufacturing company.

In 1989 Mintzberg distilled 20 years of his thinking into *Mintzberg on Management*, the best introduction to his work, which also includes a chapter on 'crafting strategy' – how this important managerial function works – and the concept that helped shape his understanding of the process, the different part played by the right and left hemispheres of the brain in managerial work.

Briefly, Mintzberg has established a theory that successful chief executives favour the right-hand or intuitive side of their brain more than the left-hand or analytical side. Creative strategy, he argues, requires 'right brain' thinking and there is more than logical planning to the effective management of an organization. 'Effective managers seem to revel in ambiguity, in complex, mysterious systems with relatively little order.'

He supports his theory with some general observations of managers at work, while emphasizing that, as a theory, it still remains largely in the realm of speculation.

Nevertheless, he is convinced that 'the important policy-level processes required to manage an organization rely to a considerable extent on the faculties identified with the brain's right hemisphere.'

And in typically iconoclastic style, he adds that if his suggestions turn out to be valid, teachers of management had better 'revise drastically some of their notions about management education. Unfortunately, the revolution in that sphere over the last 15 years – while it has brought so much of value – has virtually consecrated the modern management school to the worship of the left hemisphere . . . There is a need for a new balance in our schools, the balance that the best of human brains can achieve, between the analytic and the intuitive.'

In recent years, Mintzberg has been conducting further research on what managers do, spending time observing them at work in jobs ranging from the chief executives of Britain's National Health Service and the Royal Bank of Canada to the warden of a Canadian mountain park and the conductor of the Winnipeg Symphony Orchestra. Most leading management writers, he comments, tend to emphasize one part of the manager's job – as doer, thinker, leader, controller – to the exclusion of the others. Even in the list of tasks or roles found in classic management literature, 'the integrated work of managing still gets lost in the process of describing it.'

To overcome this, Mintzberg constructed a model of managerial activity 'from the inside out,' set out as concentric circles from 'the largely cerebral roles of conceiving and scheduling at the core to the more tangible roles of getting things done,' and then laid his fieldwork observations over this model.

'From the outside (or most tangible level) in, managers can manage action *directly*, they can manage *people* to encourage them to take the necessary actions, and they can manage *information* to influence the people in turn to take their necessary actions. In other words, the ultimate objective of managerial work, and of the functioning of any organizational unit, the taking of action, can be managed directly, indirectly through people, or even more indirectly by information through people.

'The manager can thus choose to intervene at any of the three levels, but once done, he or she must work through the remaining ones . . . the level a given manager favours becomes an important determinant of his or her managerial style, especially distinguishing so-called "doers" who prefer direct action, "leaders" who prefer working through people, and "administrators" who prefer to work by information.' ('Rounding Out the Manager's Job,' *Sloan Management Review*, Fall 1994).

In his initial study of chief executives, Mintzberg found that perhaps 40 per cent of their time was devoted exclusively to communicating, just gaining and sharing information. 'In other words, the job of managing is fundamentally one of processing information, notably by talking and especially by listening.'

The fruits of this latest research on managerial work, still ongoing in 1998, are to be incorporated in a future book.

KEY WRITINGS

Mintzberg, H. (1973, 1980) *The Nature of Managerial Work*, New York: Harper and Row.

Mintzberg, H. (1979) *The Structuring of Organizations*, New Jersey: Prentice-Hall.

Mintzberg, H. (1983) *Structures in Fives: Designing Effective Organizations*, New Jersey: Prentice-Hall.

Mintzberg, H. (1983) *Power In and Around Organizations*, New Jersey: Prentice-Hall.

Mintzberg, H. (1989) *Mintzberg on Management*, New York: The Free Press; London: Collier Macmillan.

Mintzberg, H. (1994) *The Rise and Fall of Strategic Planning*, New York: Free Press; London: Prentice-Hall.

Mintzberg, H. (1994) 'Rounding Out the Manager's Job', *Sloan Management Review*, Vol. 36, No.1.

Mintzberg, H. (1996) 'Managing Government, Governing Management', Cambridge, Mass.: *Harvard Business Review* (May/June).

Mintzberg, H. (1996) 'Musings on Management', Cambridge, Mass.: *Harvard Business Review* (July/Aug).

KENICHI OHMAE

(b. 1943)

Lessons from Japanese global business strategy

Japan's only world-class management guru, Kenichi Ohmae is the former head of McKinsey's Tokyo office and a leading international exponent of global business strategy.

Ohmae, who holds a doctorate in nuclear engineering from MIT, joined McKinsey in 1972. He has published around 30 books and articles on strategy and is renowned for the insights he offers into Japanese strategic thinking and its relationship to Japan's competitive strength in world markets.

In Ohmae's view, western management thinkers have rarely succeeded in analysing Japanese strategic management styles, focusing instead on tactics like quality circles and company songs. There is a failure, Ohmae considers, to recognize the most fundamental difference between eastern and western strategy – that Japanese companies plan for the long term, western ones for short-term profits.

Ohmae's two most influential books are *The Mind of the Strategist*, first published in 1982, and *Triad Power* (1985), in which he argued that companies which fail to establish themselves inside all three major trading blocs – Europe, the US and the Pacific Rim – become fatally vulnerable to competition from those which do so. The 'three Cs' – commitment, competitiveness and creativity – form his prescription for success in the Triad. *The Mind of the Strategist*, subtitled in its first edition 'The Art of Japanese Business', is a highly readable exploration of techniques that can be developed to match the mixture of analysis and intuition which many Japanese business leaders bring to their strategic planning.

Following the publication of *In Search of Excellence* by two of his US McKinsey colleagues, Tom Peters and Robert Waterman, Ohmae embarked on his own study of excellent companies for the Japanese market.

A colleague of Ohmae's at McKinsey summed up his approach as: 'He questions everything. He's always asking "Why?"'. His 1990 work, *The Borderless World*, reinforced his gadfly reputation with its bold contentions, among them his view that the trade imbalance between the US and Japan is an 'illusion created by accounting systems that are tragically out of date.'

In 1995 he left McKinsey to enter local politics in Tokyo, and published *The End of the Nation State*, a title that may, in the light of the armed struggles in central and eastern Europe, prove as premature as Francis Fukuyama's *The End of History*.

Of all the scores of books produced by management gurus since World War II, Kenichi Ohmae's *The Mind of the Strategist* has a good claim to be the most practical teaching aid to the development of higher management skills. His objective was to show how outstanding strategists – who in Japan often lack a formal business education – go about developing the ideas that solve problems and create opportunities for their companies. It is less a formula than a set of concepts and approaches which can help anyone to develop this valuable mental agility.

What business strategy is all about, says Ohmae, 'what distinguishes it from all other kinds of business planning, is . . . competitive advantage.' Corporate strategy, he argues, implies an attempt 'to alter a company's strength relative to that of its competitors in the most efficient way.'

Intuition and insight, in Ohmae's view, are more effective keys to successful strategy than rational analysis, though this has its place in the process. 'In what I call the mind of the strategist, insight and a consequent drive for achievement, often amounting to a sense of mission, fuel a thought process which is basically creative and intuitive rather than rational,' he writes.

He defines creative insight as 'the ability to combine, synthesize or reshuffle previously unrelated phenomena in such a way that you get more out of the emergent whole than you have put in.' If creativity cannot be taught, he maintains, it can certainly be consciously cultivated. How it can be cultivated in people with no natural talent for strategy, or in a corporate culture at odds with creative thinking, forms the core of Ohmae's book.

An earlier book, *The Corporate Strategist* (1975) attempted to do it in a specifically Japanese context. *The Mind of the Strategist* is larded with Japanese case studies – how Honda, Toyota or Matsushita, for instance, created new markets or challenged successful competitors – but its application is universal.

The book is organized under three main headings: 'The Art of Strategic Thinking', 'Building Successful Strategies', and 'Modern Strategic Realities.' The first explores the basic mental processes involved – dissecting a problem or situation into its constituent parts; asking the right 'solution-oriented' questions, constructing 'issue diagrams' and 'profit diagrams' to facilitate getting to the right diagnosis.

Ohmae identifies the 'four routes to strategic advantage' – strategy based on a company's key factors for success in its capability to increase market share and profitability; strategy based on exploiting any relative superiority; strategy based on aggressive initiatives, challenging accepted assumptions; and strategy based on 'strategic degrees of freedom' (SDF) – development of innovations such as new markets or products.

All four options are examined in depth with case studies drawn from Japanese industry. As an example of aggressive initiative, he cites Toyota's Taiichi Ohno questioning the need to stockpile large quantities of components for the production line. Ohno's question eventually led to the introduction of 'just-in-time,' and a revolution in production systems worldwide.

'If, instead of accepting the first answer, one . . . persists in asking "Why?" four or five times in succession, one will certainly get to the guts of the issue, where fundamental bottlenecks and problems lie.'

Strategic degrees of freedom also require the recognition of changes in the users' (customers') objective function (such as a preference for compact physical size in stereo equipment over performance measured by power output – part of Sony's rise in the market – or the perception by Honda and other car companies that many customers were switching from speed and prestige to convenience, economy and utility).

'Stretching one's mind to find the SDF by which the new objectives can be satisfied is one way to become a pioneer in the new-business game,' Ohmae observes.

Ohmae advises trainee strategists not to worry overmuch about details that seem to threaten their plans. Write down each point of uncertainty, he counsels, and assess its positive or negative outcome. If the overall result won't be affected by a few negative factors, follow the example of Japanese entrepreneurs such as Konosuke Matsushita and Soichiro Honda and persist with execution of the plan.

Responsiveness to changing customer objectives lies at the root of Ohmae's system for constructing a business strategy. His three points of the 'strategic triangle' are the corporation (its strengths, weaknesses and resources), the customer and the competition.

'Customer-based strategies are the basis of all strategy,' asserts Ohmae. He is convinced that a corporation's foremost concern should be the interest of its customers as opposed to that of its shareholders or other parties. 'In the long run the corporation that is genuinely interested in its customers is the one that will be interesting to investors.'

Ohmae's book goes on to analyse competitive advantage by price, volume and cost and their effect on profitability. 'If, for example, you can get a better price because of better

design, you may be able to achieve better profit performance than your competitors.'

Having set out strategic mechanisms for single businesses,
Ohmae then integrates them into a corporate structure,
looking at such techniques as Product Portfolio
Management (PPM), a corporate idea for large, diverse
businesses, based on the principles of managing an investment portfolio.

In the 'Strategic Realities' section, Ohmae set his planning process against five 'key economic trends' which he
believed would have an important impact on business
strategies in the last decade. In 1982, these were:

1. Continuing low growth
2. Market maturity and strategic stalemate
3. Uneven distribution of resources (e.g. Opec oil)
4. Growing international complexities
5. Irreversible inflation

Ohmae listed seven major changes that he thought likely to
influence business strategies in the 1990s:

1. A shift from labour-intensive to capital-intensive industries
2. A shift from multinational to 'multi-local' companies
3. A shift in the fixed to variable cost ratio
4. A shift from steel to electronics-based industries
5. A shift in business unit definition
6. A shift from international to local financial management
7. A shift to a coordinated corporate value system

Ohmae's iconoclastic books on global business strategy have
made him an international celebrity on the lecture circuit.
He says that he is now more interested in 'society, social
systems and large corporate activities on a global scale . . .
Interdependence is the key to making our world work.'

The Borderless World (1990) has an important message for
large companies in the 1990s. 'Too few managers,' says
Ohmae, 'consciously try to set plans and build organizations
as if they see all key customers equidistant from the corpo-

rate centre . . . The word "overseas" has no place in Honda's vocabulary because it sees itself as equidistant from all key customers.'

KEY WRITINGS

Ohmae, K. (1982, 1983) *The Mind of the Strategist*, New York: McGraw-Hill; London: Penguin Business Library.

Ohmae, K. (1985) *Triad Power: The Coming Shape of Global Competition*, New York: Free Press.

Ohmae, K. (1990) *The Borderless World*, New York: Harper Business; London: Collins.

Ohmae, K. (1995) *The End of the Nation State*, London: Collins.

RICHARD T. PASCALE

(b. 1938)

Continuous renewal in organizations

Leading business consultant, associate fellow of Oxford University and for 20 years a member of the faculty at Stanford University's Graduate Business School, Pascale's comparative research into US and Japanese companies in the 1970s contributed to his important role in developing, in collaboration with McKinsey's, the famous 'Seven-S' framework of guiding management concepts. Tom Peters and Robert H. Waterman Jr., who were later to deploy this tool in their record-selling book *In Search of Excellence*, were two of the McKinsey team involved.

The 'hard' S factors were strategy, structure and systems; the 'soft' S factors – at which Japanese companies excelled – were style, shared values or 'superordinate goals,' skills and staff. Superordinate goals were the hidden key to the power of the soft S factors, the glue, in Pascale's description, that held the other six parts of the framework together.

Pascale turned his research, with co-author Anthony Athos, into a hugely influential best-seller in 1981, a year ahead of *Excellence*. *The Art of Japanese Management* used the Seven-S framework to illuminate brilliantly the differences in management culture between Japan and the US, encapsulated in close-up studies of Matsushita Electric and ITT and their respective chief executives' management styles.

In the late 1980s Pascale moved to a new perspective on management priorities in a world where nothing could be safely predicted except chaos and discontinuity. His powerful book *Managing on the Edge* (1990) examined how underlying paradigms or habits of thought in organizations filter and subtly distort a full understanding of change.

A central theme of the book, which was hailed by the *Financial Times* as more intellectually stimulating than *In Search of Excellence*, is that the ultimate, largely ignored task of management is one of creating and breaking paradigms, and that success in organizations breeds failure unless there is a system in place that constantly encourages debate, even contention and conflict, leading to a process of continued renewal.

From his San Francisco base, Pascale has contributed a number of key articles to *Harvard Business Review* in recent years, as well as a BBC television series and video course on corporate transformation. As a visiting scholar at California's Santa Fe Institute, he has lately turned his attention to complex adaptive systems, the generalizable properties of all living organisms. His inquiry has revealed such principles as the tendency for living systems to self-organize, to 'surf at the edge of chaos' when faced with a complex task, and to evolve ever higher levels of complexity.

This work will form the basis of his next book, scheduled for publication in late 1998, which will tie these findings to practical steps in organizational transformation.

The Art of Japanese Management hit its moment precisely, as did *In Search of Excellence* a year later. US business leaders were increasingly worried about the growing power of Japanese companies and the competitive edge they were gaining in Western markets. The book that could crack the Japanese secret for them was bound to become a best-seller.

Pascale and Athos not only identified the reasons for

Japanese competitive excellence but what enabled organizations in Japan to continue performing to superior standards over time. The answer was the Seven S model, and how the best Japanese enterprises used the Western managerial 'hard S' levers to a more productive purpose by allying them with the 'soft S' levers.

In one of the most gripping narratives to be found in management literature, Pascale and Athos held a mirror up in turn to leading exemplars of the two business cultures – Matsushita Electric, run by its founder Konosuke Matsushita, and ITT, then managed by the formidable hard man of American business, Harold Geneen.

Like Peters and Waterman after them, Pascale and Athos found that many of the best-performing US companies that had sustained their vitality over time were just as efficient as the Japanese at synchronizing hard and soft S values. 'The best firms link their purposes and ways of realizing them to human values as well as to economic measures like profit and efficiency,' they observed.

Remarking that many observers of the Japanese phenomenon tended to view it through American cultural filters and therefore assumed the soft S factors to be mere froth, the authors produced a memorable image: 'That "froth" has the power of the Pacific.'

In particular, Pascale and Athos were the first to single out the importance of 'superordinate goals' or shared values in providing an organization with a compelling purpose or vision. This insight laid the foundation of today's concept of vision statements. The book analyses superordinate goals in relationship to the company in six different contexts:

- As an entity
- External markets
- Internal operations
- Employees
- Society and the state
- Culture, including religion

In their study of the two multinationals, Matsushita and ITT, Pascale and Athos drew comparisons in such areas as marketing, financial methods, research, strategic planning policies and – the key factor – in the styles of management practised by Konosuke Matsushita and Harold Geneen.

The authors found the US company generally comparable with the Japanese one as far as hard S factors were concerned. The crucial difference lay in the soft S areas: in consequence, they suggested, US companies tend to be wasteful of human resources while the Japanese, as is natural to their culture of interdependence and consensus, have a far more productive and collaborative boss/subordinate relationship.

The originality of the book lay in its holistic approach and cultural perspective on management. This laid the groundwork for much subsequent writing on corporate culture. *The Art of Japanese Management* continues to be essential reading.

Pascale's first major solo book, *Managing on the Edge*, is likely to prove just as important to management thinking in its time. Like Peters' *Thriving on Chaos*, it addresses the need for a radical reappraisal of conventional management wisdom, especially in the area of managing change and disruption in the business environment.

Although Pascale had worked with Peters and Waterman prior to *In Search of Excellence*, he came to feel that *Excellence* and other books like it were shallow and had resulted in a number of management fads that failed to address the needs of managers wanting to develop and maintain excellence within their organizations.

Managing on the Edge, subtitled 'How the Smartest Companies Use Conflict to Stay Ahead,' takes the decline of successful corporations as its point of departure and examines how underlying paradigms or mind-sets blind managements to the first weak signals of change. A central premise of the book is that the ultimate, and largely ignored, task of management is one of creating and breaking paradigms. Constructive use of contention, Pascale argues, coupled with persistent self-questioning, is one of the most effective ways of doing this.

Pascale's thesis is that success breeds failure unless there is a system that constantly encourages debate and thus leads to a process of continued organizational renewal. Excellent organizations often persist with perceptions formed in the period of their greatest success and never question these orthodoxies. Their great strengths become the roots of weakness because they resist change and are unable to see environmental change happening around them.

The book identifies a process of questioning and renewal that is partly organizational and partly a matter of attitude. In order to be creative and to adapt to changing circumstances, the organization needs to have controlled conflict. The book gives case examples, featuring some of America's leading multinational companies (the transformation of Ford gets 60 pages), of how organizations can foster the creative tensions necessary for renewal.

Pascale explains how certain pioneering Western and Japanese companies – he rates Honda one of the best managed companies in the world – become 'engines of inquiry,' mechanisms for continuous learning and renewal. He describes the specific mechanisms by which Honda channels the forces of constructive contention in a way that keeps the company 'in a sort of restless, uneasy state, which enables it to get a great deal out of its people and itself as an entity.'

Citicorp is cited as an example of a company that is 'living dangerously' by maintaining a 'Darwinian' culture in which jobs are always at risk and judged by each day's performance. Under Walter Wriston, who changed Citicorp's perception of its business as one of moving information rather than one of moving money, the company harnessed tension to make an aggressive impact in a staid industry. But such a level of tension, creating a lot of personal insecurity, could turn against itself if the balance were lost.

The same failure of success can occur if a company such as Hewlett-Packard takes its mission of vision and values to such lengths that they become a behavioural straitjacket. 'So if there is one prescription,' Pascale has commented, 'it is that there is no prescription. Or that any prescription taken to extremes is going to cause trouble.'

Pascale's next book, arising from his work at the Santa Fe Institute on complex adaptive systems, will provide grounded practices that have been tested and proven in organizations such as Sears, Royal Dutch Shell and the US

Army. These exemplify how the organization of the next century will tap distributed intelligence, harness rather than resist turbulence in the environment and radically alter the meaning of leadership. Pascale offers seven key disciplines which will enable organizations to reinvent themselves on a continuous basis.

KEY WRITINGS

Pascale, R. T. and Athos, A. (1981, 1982, 1986) *The Art of Japanese Management*, New York: Simon and Schuster; London: Allen Lane; Penguin Books
Pascale, R. T. (1990) *Managing on the Edge*, New York: Simon and Schuster; London: Viking.
Pascale, R. T., Goss, T. and Athos, A. (1993) 'The Reinvention Roller Coaster', Cambridge, Mass.: *Harvard Business Review* (Nov/Dec).
Pascale, R. T., Millemann, M. and Gioja, L. (1997) 'Changing the Way We Change', Cambridge, Mass.: *Harvard Business Review* (Nov/Dec).

TOM PETERS AND ROBERT H. WATERMAN JR

(b.1942) (b.1936)

The 'excellence' cult and prescriptions for managing chaotic change

Tom Peters and Robert Waterman will forever be linked because of the phenomenal success of *In Search of Excellence*, although it was the only book the two former McKinsey consultants wrote together. Since its publication in 1982, each has carved out his own distinctive niche in authorship and on the lecture trail.

Excellence is by far the world's best-selling business book. It was slow to take off on both sides of the Atlantic, but its reputation rocketed by word of mouth and suddenly companies were ordering '50, 100, 200 copies to give to their executives,' as the British publisher recalls. It reached the million mark in sales in record time, within a year, and has now sold over 5m copies. Despite the fact that two-thirds of its 'excellent' companies have since faded in performance – Peters began his 1987 book *Thriving on Chaos* with the bold words, 'There are no excellent companies' – *In Search of Excellence* still endlessly reprints in paperback and it continues to walk off the airport bookstalls where most business books are sold in the UK.

Before joining McKinsey in 1974, Peters worked in the Pentagon for two years, where he became 'fascinated by complex organizations.' He then took a master's degree in civil engineering at Cornell University before serving in Vietnam. Later, he took an MBA at Stanford and worked again in Washington for the Office of Management and Budget. Today, he and Michael Porter can probably claim to be the most sought-after and expensive management lecturers in the world. The Tom Peters Group has built a huge business in videos, cassettes and TV series as well as personal appearances and consultancy work.

Bob Waterman is the complete temperamental opposite of the excitable, hyper-active Peters, whose shirts are rapidly soaked with sweat as he delivers his quickfire, floor-pacing lectures. A tall, laid-back Californian, Waterman says he could, if he chose, do as many lectures as Peters – roughly one every other day – but he observes laconically: 'Why kill myself?' Running his own consultancy in San Mateo, outside San Francisco, for two days a week, giving a couple of dozen lectures a year and acting as a director of several companies, including a multinational power producer, suits him better than Peters' hectic travelling schedule.

The continuing royalties from *Excellence* and his corporate work give him the financial freedom, he says, to do what he wants, and he has started a career counselling business with his wife Judy, along with developing a computerized self-evaluation system to enable people to learn more about their true motivations and skills.

Waterman spent 21 years with McKinsey, initially working on the restructuring and decentralization of large organizations. He worked in Japan and Australia and in 1976 returned to San Francisco, where the partnership with Peters began. Both men left the firm after *Excellence* was published – Peters first, then Waterman in 1986 – and although they considered another co-authorship, McKinsey was not enthusiastic once Peters had left, so Peters wrote the sequel, *A Passion for Excellence*, with Nancy Austin.

Peters' work took a new direction with *Thriving on Chaos* (1987), which inaugurated a genre of books on managing change. He has since led the movement to flatter, nimbler organizational structures and preached the virtue of the virtual company in books such as *Liberation*

Management (1992), *In Pursuit of Wow!* (1994) and *The Tom Peters Seminar: Crazy Times Call for Crazy Organizations* (1994). His latest book, *Circles of Innovation* (1997), is his most eccentric yet, laid out in the style of seminar slides with a great deal of Peters' verbal gimmicks such as 'Yikes!' and words inexplicably separated into their component letters by hyphens.

Waterman's more conservative approach produced *The Renewal Factor* in 1987 and *The Frontiers of Excellence* in 1994, which developed some of the ideas from *In Search of Excellence*, chiefly the principle of learning from best practice, but which also focused on the need for managers to ride and manage change and to put people first. Waterman maintains today that the principles laid down in *Excellence* are still valid and that the claim that two-thirds of the companies faltered is based on the decline of stockmarket prices, which were at a high when the book came out.

In hindsight, he says, he would have chosen a different group of companies, but some, such as General Electric, 3M, Merck and Intel, continue fully to justify the 'excellent' tag. In any case, he points out, he and Peters observed in the book that 'many of our excellent companies probably will not stay buoyant for ever' – a comment that subsequent critics conveniently overlooked.

Waterman's own favourite management reading includes what he calls the 'heavy-duty' theoretical works of Karl Weick on organizations, Alfred Chandler's *Strategy and Structure*, the work of Chester Barnard, Elton Mayo's Hawthorne experiments ('he showed that just paying attention to things gets more done'), Drucker's *Managing for Results*, Mintzberg on how managers spend their time, and Warren Bennis, especially his earlier works on organizational development ('a little like Drucker but more theoretical').

Another book that influenced him was James Gleick's *Chaos*, a brilliant *tour de force* on the unpredictable nature of life. 'It's important stuff, an entirely new branch of mathematics. It's as if calculus were re-invented. It has a lot to say about the inherent unforecastability of things, and why things we put a lot of faith in don't work. It has a lot to say about stock markets.'

Waterman believes that F.W. Taylor's work has been 'something of a touchstone' and that we are 'still living in a world created by Taylor; the specialization of work, mechanizing things, dividing work up into functions.' However much they would deny it, he suggests, many – if not most – managers are still Taylorists at heart.

While Peters drives frenetically on round the management circuit, Waterman says in his laid-back way: 'I've said pretty much all I have to say about business management.' He is now developing ideas in a different area, that of the environment and natural resources. But he expresses satisfaction that his participation as a director of companies gives him a welcome practical touchstone for his management theories, 'to see if the stuff really works.'

Peters and Waterman have almost branded the word 'excellence' as a branch of management theory. Their phenomenally successful book has spawned a host of imitators and was the subject of a fascinated study by Japan's Kenichi Ohmae, also a McKinsey man. At the time, though, Waterman says they had no idea it would prove such a watershed.

Its simple idea was the extension of a McKinsey project begun in 1977, to analyse the lessons from 43 of *Fortune*'s top 500 companies that had consistently beaten their competitors over 20 years by six financial yardsticks:

• Compound asset growth
• Compound equity growth
• Ratio of market value to book value
• Return on capital
• Return on equity
• Return on sales

Peters and Waterman developed the famous McKinsey

171

'Seven-S' formula to analyse an organization: structure, strategy, systems, style of management, skills (corporate strengths), staff and shared values. Applying this framework to their 43 companies, they identified their eight by now well-known characteristics shared by all of them:

- A bias for action: getting on with it
- Close to the customer: learning from the people they serve
- Autonomy and entrepreneurship: fostering innovation and nurturing 'champions'
- Productivity through people; treating the rank and file as a source of quality
- Hands-on, value-driven: management showing its commitment
- Stick to the knitting: stay with the business you know
- Simple form, lean staff: some of the best companies have a minimum of headquarters staff
- Simultaneous loose-tight properties; autonomy in shop floor activities plus centralized values

All their 43 companies, Peters and Waterman found, were 'brilliant on the basics.' Also, in almost every case, a strong leader had been influential at some stage in forming the culture of excellence.

Five years after the book's publication, two-thirds of those companies had hit trouble in varying degrees, among them Atari, Avon, Wang and DuPont. Only 14 could still be classified as excellent by the original criteria.

Peters and Waterman individually concluded that nothing in today's chaotic business environment stays the same long enough for excellence of the sustained type possible before 1982 to be developed. In *Thriving on Chaos* Peters cited IBM – 'declared dead in 1979, the best of the best in 1982, and dead again in 1986.' People Express, one star of their book, collapsed completely.

Excellence, suggested P&W, required re-defining – excellent firms were now those that believed only in constant improvement and the demands of constant change.

A key concept behind *Thriving on Chaos*, a title that struck a chord with many gurus in the late 1980s, was the need to move from a hierarchical management pyramid to a horizontal, fast, cross-functional, cooperative one.

Peters evolved 45 precepts for managers of every level. They ran as follows:

- Specialize/create niches/differentiate
- Provide top quality
- Become a service addict
- Achieve total customer responsiveness
- Become true internationalists, both small and large firms
- Strive to achieve uniqueness
- Listen to customers, end users, suppliers, retailers
- Make manufacturing the prime marketing tool
- 'Over-invest' in people, frontline sales, service, distribution (make these the company heroes)
- Become customer-obsessed
- Develop an innovation strategy
- Use multi-function teams for all development activities
- Substitute pilots and prototypes for proposals
- Ignore 'Not Invented Here'; practise 'creative swiping'
- Use systematic word of mouth for launching
- Applaud champions
- Symbolize innovativeness
- Support failures by publicly rewarding well thought-out mistakes
- Measure innovation
- Make innovation a way of life for everyone
- Involve all personnel in virtually everything
- Organize as much as possible around teams
- Listen/celebrate/recognize
- Invest time in recruiting
- Invest in human capital as much as hardware
- Provide bold financial incentives for all
- Guarantee continuous employment for a large slice of the workforce
- Radically reduce layers of management
- Re-conceive middle managers as facilitators instead of guardians
- Reduce and simplify paperwork and bureaucratic procedures

- Challenge conventional management wisdom on a day-to-day basis
- Develop and live an 'enabling and empowering vision' (effective leadership at all levels is marked by a core philosophy [values] and a vision of how the enterprise or department wishes to make its mark)
- Lead by personal example
- Practise visible management
- Become a compulsive listener
- Ensure that frontline people know they are the heroes
- Examine each act of delegation and increase it radically
- Pursue horizontal management
- Focus on exactly what you have changed recently – what your subordinates have changed
- Create a sense of urgency
- Develop simple systems to encourage participation and understanding
- Simplify control systems (e.g. performance appraisals, setting of objectives, job descriptions)
- Share information with everyone
- Set conservative financial targets
- Demand total integrity in all dealings, both inside and outside the firm

Waterman's prescriptions for renewing vitality and performance in *The Renewal Factor* numbered just eight:

- Informed opportunism: 'The renewing companies treat information as their main strategic advantage, and flexibility as their main strategic weapon'
- Direction and empowerment: 'The renewing companies treat everyone as a source of creative input . . . Their managers define the boundaries and their people figure out the best way of doing the job within these boundaries'
- Friendly facts, congenial controls: 'The renewing companies treat facts as friends and financial controls as liberating'
- A different mirror: ability to step outside the company and look at it from a different perspective

- Teamwork, trust, politics and power: the first two are common to all renewing companies, the last two never found
- Causes and commitment: 'Commitment results from management's ability to turn grand causes into small actions so everyone can contribute'
- Attitudes and attention: 'Visible management attention, rather than exhortation, gets things done'
- Stability in motion: renewing companies have a 'habit of habit-breaking'

Peters and Waterman together were responsible for popularizing the study of management to a mass readership, and initiating a new direction in management thinking. No other authors have come near their feat with *Excellence* in the number of copies sold. They illuminated many issues, such as corporate culture and values, which are just as valid today as in 1982. As the business environment changed and became subject to more shocks and discontinuities, they responded with their individual views of managing change – a concept that few companies understood a decade ago, but which is now central to industrial survival.

KEY WRITINGS

Peters, T. and Waterman, R. H. Jr. (1982) *In Search of Excellence*, New York and London: Harper and Row.

Peters, T. and Austin, N. (1985) *A Passion for Excellence*, London: Collins.

Peters, T. (1987) (1988) *Thriving on Chaos*, New York: Alfred A. Knopf; London: Macmillan.

Waterman, R. H. Jr. (1987) *The Renewal Factor*, New York: Bantam.

Peters, T. (1992) *Liberation Management*, New York: Alfred A. Knopf; London: Macmillan.

Peters, T. (1994) *The Tom Peters Seminar: Crazy Times Call for Crazy Organizations*, New York: Vintage; London:

Macmillan.

Peters, T. (1994) *The Pursuit of Wow!*, New York: Vintage; London: Macmillan.

Waterman, R. H. Jr. (1994) *The Frontiers of Excellence*, London: Nicholas Brealey Publishing.

Peters, T. (1997) *Circles of Innovation*, London: Hodder and Stoughton.

MICHAEL PORTER

(b. 1947)

Strategies for competitive advantage, both national and international

Harvard Business School's star professor (of business administration) and regarded by many leading US business-men as the world's greatest expert on strategies for com-petitive advantage. With stratospheric lecture fees and books on competitive strategy that have gone into scores of printings, Porter is the most fashionable and sought-after of the younger gurus on the international circuit, rivalled only by Tom Peters, co-founder of the 'excellence' cult.

In the summer of 1990, *Business Week* described Porter as 'a business phenomenon in his own right' and 'one of the highest-paid academics anywhere.' He is booked for lectures six months in advance and has sold millions of dollars' worth of video seminars. The consultancy he co-founded occupies him four days a month, advising big-name companies. Porter himself acknowledges that he has become a 'brand' for which buyers are willing to pay.

Porter joined the Harvard faculty at the age of 26 after earning an economics doctorate there. Earlier, at Prince-ton, he had graduated in aeronautical engineering and reached professional standard at golf. His first book, *Competitive Strategy* (1980), is in its 52nd printing and is deemed by many on both sides of the Atlantic to be the definitive work on corporate strategy. His last to date, *The Competitive Advantage of Nations*, analyses the reasons for ten countries' ability to gain global market share in certain

industries. (The UK comes out with a depressingly periph-
eral list, aside from chemicals and pharmaceuticals: Porter
deems it a world leader, for example, in auctioneering and
biscuit manufacture. Britain scores only seven world-chal-
lenging categories to Switzerland's 16 and Denmark's 11.)

Porter's next book, his first for nearly a decade, will
'redefine the thinking and practice of competitive strategy
as we know it.'

The very words 'competitive strategy' or 'competitive
advantage' are enough to identify Michael Porter wherever
management gurus gather. Some critics claim that his ideas
for analysing markets and industries are based on old economic theories, and Porter himself has acknowledged his
debt to Joseph A. Schumpeter, among others, in *The
Competitive Advantage of Nations*. What he does brilliantly,
however, is to package and simplify analytical models that
would otherwise be dauntingly difficult for most working
businessmen to understand. His seminars, in particular, are
as lively as those of Tom Peters.

On joining the Harvard faculty, Porter was among the
first to project corporate strategy in marketplace terms
rather than as a theoretical concept linking various functions
in an organization.

His basic tool for managers seeking to analyse their own
company's competitive position employs five factors or
forces that drive competition:

• Existing rivalry between firms
• The threat of new entrants to a market
• The threat of substitute products and services
• The bargaining power of suppliers
• The bargaining power of buyers

He then identifies five generic descriptions of industries:
fragmented, emerging, mature, declining and global.

Porter says a firm may possess two kinds of competitive

advantage: low cost or differentiation. 'Competitive advantage is a function of either providing comparable buyer value more efficiently than competitors (low cost), or performing activities at comparable cost but in unique ways that create more buyer value than competitors and, hence, command a premium price (differentiation).'

Firms that operate in a number of different countries can locate processes where the best advantage lies – e.g. low labour costs, or proximity to vast markets like Japanese firms based in the UK – but at the same time, Porter argues, the most competitive ones come from home bases that are themselves strong and competitive. This sharpens up the instinct to succeed and provides valuable 'cluster' support from equally successful linked industries that act as buyers and suppliers.

This theory, developed over several books and numerous articles, reaches its full flowering in *The Competitive Advantage of Nations*, which takes as its key a 'diamond' of factors that makes some nations (and consequently their industries) more competitive than others.

The four points of this diamond are:

- *Factor conditions*: the nation's position in factors of production (such as skilled labour or infrastructure) necessary to compete in a particular industry
- *Demand conditions*: the nature of home demand for the industry's product or service and how discriminating it is
- *Related and supporting industries*: the presence or absence of supplier industries and related industries that are internationally competitive themselves
- *Company strategy, structure and rivalry*: the conditions governing how firms are created, organized and managed, as well as the nature of domestic rivalry. Tough domestic rivalry breeds international success

Firms gain competitive advantage outside their home markets, Porter argues, when their own countries provide a dynamic competitive environment, characterized by an accumulation of specialized assets and skills and a constant stimulus to upgrade and improve their products and processes. 'Clusters' of mutually supporting industries are important to success; one reason why Britain's performance has declined over the years.

Among Porter's strategic recommendations for the competitive company are:

- Sell to the most sophisticated and demanding buyers: they will set a standard for the organization
- Seek out buyers with the most difficult needs; they become part of a firm's R&D programme
- Establish norms of exceeding the toughest regulatory hurdles or product standards: these provide targets that will force improvement
- Source from the most advanced and international home-based suppliers; those with competitive advantage already will challenge the firm to improve and upgrade
- Treat employees as permanent instead of a demoralizing hire-and-fire approach
- Establish outstanding competitors as motivators

One of Porter's favourite methods of identifying a firm's competitive position is to analyse its 'value chain' – all the activities it performs and how they interact. Examining these components sheds light on the roots of costs and how they behave, and picks out existing and potential sources of differentiation. 'A firm gains competitive advantage by performing these strategically important activities more cheaply or better than its competitors.'

Kathryn Rudie Harrigan, a former student of Porter's – and now a guru in her own right as well as being professor of strategic management at New York's Columbia University – says the ideas in *Competitive Strategy* are required reading in every US business school and most executive education programmes. 'The framework he popularized forms the cornerstone for the next decade of research concerning strategy formulation . . . . The first chapter of the book he edited about global competition* provides what has become the dominant framework for looking at issues in global strategy.'

*Competition in Global Industries, ed. by M. E. Porter (Harvard Business School Press, 1986).

KEY WRITINGS

Porter, M. E. (1980) *Competitive Strategy: Techniques for Analysing Industries and Competitors*, New York: Free Press.
Porter, M. E. (1985) *Competitive Advantage*, New York: Free Press.
Porter, M. E. (ed) (1986) *Competition in Global Industries*, Cambridge, Mass.: Harvard Business School Press.
Porter, M. E. (1990) *The Competitive Advantage of Nations*, London: Macmillan.

REG REVANS

(b. 1907)

Managers educating each other through 'Action Learning'

Underrated British (Southampton-born) inventor of 'Action Learning,' in which working teams of managers educate each other amid the real risk, confusion and opportunity of the workplace itself. The idea has become an accepted part of management education, though only the Japanese have fully acknowledged the importance of Revans' early work – as a foundation stone of their quality circle philosophy.

Revans, a one-time local government official working in the educational field, is known to feel bitter about his position as a guru without honour in his own country. Management consultant Bob Garratt, who worked with Revans in industry, says his theories form 'one of the few bodies of management work which are highly scientifically and mathematically based, beautifully researched.' Garratt suspects it was this that 'frightened people off,' especially in the late 1960s and early 1970s when British management education came heavily under the influence of US West Coast psychotherapy and the whole humanist, sociological approach to industry. But the theory still 'works wonderfully', says Garratt.

Revans' ideas have played an important role in management training in continental Europe. A programme in Belgium based on Revans' theories was described as being partly responsible for Belgium's 102-per-cent increase in industrial productivity between 1971 and 1981. (For comparison, Japan's figure is 85 per cent and Britain's 28 per cent.)

In the 1970s Revans became president of the European Association of Management Training Centres, and an EC report later paid tribute to his work (*Education in the European Community*, 1978).

Revans said of his book *Action Learning* (1974) that he bought most of the copies as scrap. It did not sell, yet it was the culmination of some 40 years' working and thinking by Revans, who wrote his first paper on training in 1938, when he was responsible for technical and professional education on Essex County Council.

Over the next 20 years he developed the radical theory that managers learned better from each other in working management situations than they ever could in a classroom. The message was driven home for him while working in a training and development capacity in the coal-mining industry, where he observed how miners had to 'carry the educational can' in working with young newcomers to the pits. They had to combine the teaching of technical knowledge with sensitivity to the fears and insecurity of youngsters working underground for the first time.

Revans identified these abilities as essential to the manager of any large enterprise. In doing so, as one appreciation of his work puts it, he 'became a forerunner of the whole socio-technical school of management which was to blossom in the 1960s.'

From his observations in the pits, Revans concluded that miners and managers should also learn from and with each other, and he proposed the formation of a Staff College through which people in the industry with common problems could be brought together to exchange ideas for practical solutions. This was the core of Action Learning, which Revans later took into National Health Service hospitals.

Revans also studied the effect of the size of a business on

the morale of people working for it, and concluded well ahead of E. F. Schumacher (a colleague of his on the Coal Board) that 'small is beautiful.'

'What does make Revans unique,' wrote Ronald Lessem of City University Business School, 'is the way he has linked together industrial relations (artisan and scribe), human relations (self and others), technological change (education and industry), and the whole question of scale (centre and periphery) with information processing, problem-solving and learning.'

Revans, said Lessem, 'placed at the centre of things the "springs of human action." It is one's perception of the problem, he said, one's evaluation of what is to be gained by solving it, and one's estimate of the resources at hand to solve it, that supply these action springs.'

Revans sees the concept as one of great antiquity, citing Buddha as 'an early believer in action learning, teaching others that it is from their own real experiences that the most fundamental truths are most likely to be learned.'

He has always taken a holistic approach, incorporating some elements of religious belief, to the practice of management. His synthesis of tasks and relationships, personal consciousness and management technique, organizational science and religious faith was distilled into *The Theory of Practice in Management* (1966). This was followed by *Developing Effective Managers* (1971), in which Revans set out a model for achieving managerial objectives, based on three systems – Alpha, Beta and Gamma. System Alpha is concerned with the manager's use of information in designing strategies; System Beta with achieving them by negotiation and System Gamma with monitoring the learning curve of adapting to experience and change.

Young, fast-track managers have responded to Action Learning more than the older generation. One of the few leading British industrialists who did recognize its practical value was Arnold (now Lord) Weinstock of GEC. Action learning has been practised in Egypt, Africa and India, and became part of many management training programmes. In February 1988 Sir Douglas Hague wrote: 'We are in a new industrial revolution which requires management trainers to develop "action learning" from real experience within business and industry, rather than getting tied up with theory and academia.'

Revans has been quoted as saying: 'The facts now are that all I have been on about these fifty years is slowly being seen to have been right' (*Makers of Management*, by David Clutterbuck and Stuart Crainer, 1990). He remains convinced that action learning is an idea whose time has come – even if his own national peers should be among the last to appreciate it.

KEY WRITINGS

Revans, R. W. (1966) *The Theory of Practice in Management*, London: Macdonald.
Revans, R. W. (1971) *Developing Effective Managers*.
Revans, R. W. (1979) *Action Learning*, London: Blond and Briggs.

(It is indicative of Revans' prophet-without-honour fate that a 1982 symposium of papers on his theories, published under the title *The Origins and Growth of Action Learning*, should have been published by Studentlitteratur in West Germany under the auspices of the Bratt Institut fur Neues Lernen and available in an English language version from a small Bromley firm called Chartwell-Bratt. All Revans' books are difficult to obtain outside libraries.)

EDGAR H. SCHEIN

(b. 1928)

The 'psychological contract' between employer and employee

American social psychologist and Professor of Management at the Sloan School of Management, Massachusetts Institute of Technology, who coined the term 'the psychological contract' to express the unwritten understandings that exist within an organization.

Schein virtually invented the concept of corporate culture – the commonly held set of assumptions about an organization's values and practices – which has only recently attracted substantial attention from management writers.

Schein worked at MIT with Douglas McGregor (qv) of 'Theory X and Theory Y' fame, and was greatly influenced by him. Britain's Charles Handy (qv) studied under Schein, Warren Bennis (qv) and Chris Argyris (qv) and has said the experience 'transformed my life.'

Edgar Schein is responsible for two coinages that have entered the language of management thinking – the 'psychological contract' and the 'career anchor.' Both are intimately connected with the analysis of motivation, which is the root of Schein's work.

The first embraces what an employee expects from those

who employ him or her, not only in economic terms like pay, conditions, hours and job security, but also how he or she is treated and encouraged to develop abilities and responsibility. Schein believes that many strikes and industrial disputes occur basically because this contract has been broken, even though the flashpoint may appear to be a specific economic grievance. The psychological contract is not one-sided; it also includes a company's expectations about the people who work for it, such as loyalty and diligence. It is essential for both aspects to match or correspond if the 'contract' is to work on a long-term basis.

Allied to this is the career anchor: the perceptions about themselves that individuals hold in a particular organization, and which encourage them to remain in that organization. These relate strongly to self-esteem and satisfaction with the way talents are allowed to develop, and tend to be moulded by experience in the early part of an organizational career.

Schein identified these as typical career anchors: how individuals viewed their technical competence, managerial competence, security and autonomy in the job they were doing. Career anchors can also, he explained, have a narrowing effect on a person's development even within an organization in which he or she seems content: for example, a graduate's view of his technical competence was such that he saw himself doing technical work only instead of expanding in mid-career into managerial responsibility.

The assumptions that individuals develop about themselves within their organization are in turn largely shaped by the assumptions those organizations hold about their own values, goals and how things are done, which they pass on in various ways to their employees.

These form a company's culture and may emerge in all kinds of ways, from the sober suits and white shirts that IBM salesmen were traditionally expected to wear to the intellectual clubbiness and sense of belonging that typify many departments within the BBC – always known simply as 'the Corporation' to its career staff. (ICI has a similar 'family' culture, and at one time its historic Mond Division, now subsumed in the restructuring of the late 1980s, had its own culture within ICI based on its leading-edge achievements in scientific innovation.)

Schein says an organization's culture is 'what it has learned as a total social unit over the course of its history.' He defines it as made up of artefacts (dress codes, office layouts, the signals a stranger would pick up); values (often enshrined in anecdotes from the founder's time); and underlying assumptions (behaviour within the organization and of the organization in the environment outside).

Consensus on such cultural landmarks among both workforce and management is essential to successful achievement of the organization's goals. Schein outlines five key areas in which this consensus should operate:

- The mission – 'what business are we in, and why?'
- The goals, which should include specific goals for all workers
- The means to accomplish the goals, including reward and incentive systems
- The means of measuring progress, including reporting and feedback
- The strategies for what to do when things go wrong

Schein's belief that the key to successful leadership is managing cultural change in an organization has made him the guru for a rapidly growing band of writers on corporate culture and how it affects, for example, the success or failure of a takeover or merger of two companies with differing cultures, or the diversification of a company into new markets. Schein designed a set of diagnostic steps to help identify such cultural and compatibility problems and suggest ways of solving them.

Diagnostic ability, indeed, is an essential attribute of good management, in Schein's view. His whole work on the roots of motivation began, like that of his mentor Douglas McGregor, by analysing the way managers view the people they manage.

Historically, these models divide into three. There is the 'rational-economic' model held by F. W. Taylor and expressed by McGregor as 'Theory X' – basically, the view that most people have to be coerced into work by economic incentives and require constant management supervision. Then there is the 'social' model, formulated by Mayo and his Hawthorne experiments, which recognized needs other than economic and the importance of a worker's peer groups on performance. The third historical concept, the 'self-actualizing' model, developed the social model further, into understanding the needs of individuals to develop their full potential. Abraham Maslow (qv) with his 'hierarchy of needs'; McGregor with Theory Y; Argyris (qv) and Herzberg (qv) were other influential gurus in this field. To these existing models, Schein added a fourth – the 'complex' model. This argued that in the huge gamut of human needs and motivations, an individual's response will be governed by many variables at different times and in different situations. Schein also examined how incentives change according to an individual's changing perceptions; for example, why millionaires and other achievers persist in seeking still more millions or in setting themselves new and more difficult goals.

Robert Browning's lines: 'A man's reach should exceed his grasp, Or what's a heaven for?' encapsulate the mystery of motivation which Edgar Schein's work sets out to unravel.

KEY WRITINGS

Schein, E. H. (1978) *Career Dynamics: Matching Individual and Organizational Needs*, Wokingham: Addison-Wesley.
Schein, E. H. (1980) *Organizational Psychology*, New Jersey: Prentice-Hall.
Schein, E. H. (1985) *Organizational Culture and Leadership*, San Francisco: Jossey-Bass.

RICHARD J. SCHONBERGER

(b. 1937)

Each function in a business seen as a 'customer' of the next in the chain

American industrial engineer and now international consultant and lecturer, who is credited with introducing just-in-time and other Japanese manufacturing techniques to the US. After leaving college, he worked for eight years in US defence industries – shipbuilding, aircraft overhaul, army tank manufacturing. He then took a PhD in business studies at the University of Nebraska, specializing in production management and information systems, subsequently teaching there for 13 years.

At this time, he recalls, 'I was disgusted with manufacturing and thought the future lay with management information systems. I dropped it like a hot potato when manufacturing got exciting again.'

The catalyst in manufacturing happened through his work with computers in industry. Material Requirements Planning (MRP) was, he says, 'the only exciting thing to have happened in manufacturing in 50 years.'

Schonberger's first book, *Japanese Manufacturing Techniques* (1982), has sold over 150,000 copies in nine languages. His second, *World Class Manufacturing* (1986), sold 100,000 copies in eight languages, and together they are the two best-selling books of all time on manufacturing. Each of his five books has grown out of its predecessor, the fourth – *Building a Chain of Customers* (1990) – developing his ultimate theory that 'world class' excellence in manufacturing and service industries can only be achieved by regarding each function in a business as a 'customer' of the one serving it.

A workaholic lecturer who is now also consultant and trainer to many leading multinational corporations including Hewlett-Packard, IBM, 3M, Ford, Monsanto, DuPont, Philips and Zanussi, Schonberger visits at least one factory a week in the US or Europe. He claims that he never repeats an idea he has previously expounded. 'If I don't have something new to say, I'm not saying it.' Considering that he has published over 100 articles as well as three major books and two 'casebooks,' this must make him unique among management gurus.

Asked to distil his life's work into a 'mission statement,' Richard Schonberger replies: 'World class excellence is continual improvement in serving the customer's four basic wants: ever-better quality, ever-lower costs, ever-increasing flexibility and ever-quicker response. And that includes the next process in all the processes in between, all the way to the final customer.'

This is what Schonberger, the evangelist of 'customer-driven performance,' means by the title of *Building a Chain of Customers*. In his vividly argued theories, spattered with examples and chatty miniature case studies, the many links between and within the different functions of a business – design, manufacturing, accounting, marketing – form a continuous 'chain of customers' leading directly to those who buy the final product or service. Tom Peters has called the concept 'a bold and meticulously detailed blueprint for redesigning corporations to destroy functional myopia, to live as a whole to serve the customer.'

Schonberger says of the techniques his books expound: 'They are easy to learn, don't cost much and immediately make people feel better about their jobs. Once people begin thinking that way, they cannot define their performance any other way except in the eyes of the "customer" where their work goes next.' With this simplicity, Schonberger argues that it does not take long to train existing people in industry in how to improve rapidly, 'how to love to improve and change, and become customer-focused.'

One of the major themes in his Japanese book, published in 1982, was that the Japanese success was not due to any cultural factors; that anyone could learn the techniques of Total Quality Management and so on. Studying the results as they became practised in hundreds of firms in North America between 1982 and 1986, Schonberger derived the basis of his second book, *World Class Manufacturing*. Hewlett-Packard, which sets forth its operational philosophy in a booklet called *The HP Way*, emerged as the best example anywhere. In 1996, Schonberger carried his research further in *World Class Manufacturing: the Next Decade*, which offered a set of metrics and customer-focused principles gleaned from the world's best manufacturing companies.

Cellular manufacturing is one of Schonberger's keys to the internal customer chain. In this, clusters of people and operations are arranged according to the work flow rather than departmental requirements. He credits its invention to five British industrial pioneers between about 1965 and 1975 – Professors John L. Burbidge and G. A. B. Edwards; consultant Joseph Gombinski and works managers Gordon Ranson and Charles Allen. (Allen was manager of a Ferranti defence plant in Edinburgh that converted to the cell principle between 1968 and 1971.)

As usual, however, it was left to others to exploit and develop a brilliant British concept and to apply it to industrial practice on the shop floor.

'Toyota took those ideas, polished and perfected them and forced them on first- and second-echelon suppliers,' recalls Schonberger. 'The whole Toyota family of companies reorganized itself, moved all its machines into cells and built all its new plants according to the way the product flowed, instead of by departments.

'By and large, we owe a debt of gratitude to the Japanese for showing the power of these ideas, even though there were plenty of other people who were aware of it.'

Schonberger believes his 'customer-driven message' applies

to everyone in an organization 'from the CEO to the janitor.' When lecturing for his World Class International consultancy, he often prefers to address the 'up and coming, new blood, next crop of leaders,' rather than existing top management.

'I believe the future is in the hands of the doers – the operators, assemblers, clerks, stock handlers, drivers, servers . . . The message – how to become a world-class organization – certainly does not go over anyone's head.

'It won't be a disaster if CEOs and presidents don't read books such as mine; their lieutenants and lower-level managers, and even some of their operators do, and they will run the show right half a generation from now – if not much sooner – with or without the blessings of their high-level bosses.'

Schonberger is encouraged by the growing 'convergence' he perceives in management thinking, by how similar themes of serving the customers and involving the employees are struck in most of the recent path-setting works: he cites Tom Peters' *Thriving on Chaos*, Stanley Davis' *Future Perfect* and Grayson and O'Dell's *American Business: A Two-Minute Warning*. The voices championing the new belief in both controlling the causes of costs and focusing on the customer's primary wants (quality, throughput time, flexibility and cost) are now diverse and international, and Schonberger can claim to be among the pioneers.

KEY WRITINGS

Schonberger, R. J. (1982) *Japanese Manufacturing Techniques*, New York: The Free Press.
Schonberger, R. J. (1986) *World Class Manufacturing*, New York: The Free Press.
Schonberger, R. J. (1987) *World Class Manufacturing Casebook*, New York: The Free Press.
Schonberger, R. J. (1990) *Building a Chain of Customers*, New York: The Free Press; London: Business Books.
Schronberger, R. J. (1996) *World Class Manufacturing: The Next Decade*, New York: Free Press

E. F. SCHUMACHER

(1911–1977)

'Small is beautiful': the human scale against corporate 'giantism'

German-born economist who worked for Britain's National Coal Board for 20 years from 1950, and became famous for one idea, owed chiefly to a brilliant 'selling' title coined by his publisher. The title *Small is Beautiful* came to symbolize the whole 1970s/1980s revolt against large, impersonal organizations, yet the concept of re-thinking the conduct of business, economics and government on a small, human scale was only one of a number of ideas in Schumacher's collection of essays, published in 1973 and subtitled 'A Study of Economics As If People Mattered.'

In two or three of his 19 essays Schumacher castigated what he called 'the idolatry of giantism,' whether applied to multinational business corporations, megalopolitan urban developments or the size of nations and their internal markets, and noted that the achievement of Alfred Sloan at General Motors was 'to structure this gigantic firm in such a manner that it became, in fact, a federation of fairly reasonably sized firms.'

Surprisingly, perhaps, he also cited his own organization, the National Coal Board, one of the biggest firms, albeit publicly owned, in Western Europe, as an example where 'something very similar (to Sloan's approach) was attempted under the chairmanship of Lord Robens; strenuous efforts were made to evolve a structure which would maintain the unity of one big organization and at the same time create the "climate" or feeling of there being a federation of numerous "quasi-firms". The monolith was transformed into a well co-ordinated assembly of lively, semi-autonomous units, each with its own drive and sense of achievement.

'While many theoreticians – who may not be too closely in touch with real life – are still engaging in the idolatry of large size, with practical people in the actual world there is a tremendous longing and striving to profit, if at all possible, from the convenience, humanity and manageability of smallness.'

Schumacher's prescriptions did not go much beyond such broad-brush statements (indeed, elsewhere in his book he argues quite passionately for the virtues of nationalized industry, not usually associated with the 'small is beautiful' movement), yet his approach – philosophical, influenced by eastern religions such as Buddhism, and linked to the fulfil-ment and happiness of human beings in their working and social contexts – struck a resonant chord that reverberated long after the contents of his modest essays were forgotten. He was ahead of his time by about 15 years in advising the recognition of people's need to be involved in decision-making in small units: in the late 1980s Rosabeth Moss Kanter and other gurus would call it 'empowerment' and write whole books about it. Charles Handy says Schumacher has been 'enormously influential in spite of himself,' but today it seems incredible that so much fame could have been built on such slender foundations. Even President Jimmy Carter is said to have read and been influ-enced by Schumacher's book.

As well as his work for the Coal Board, Schumacher set up the International Technology Development Group and became an adviser on economic problems to Third World countries. He always advocated small-scale production tech-niques and said 'organizations should imitate nature, which doesn't allow a single cell to become too large.'

KEY WRITING

Schumacher, E. F. (1973) *Small is Beautiful*, London: Blond & Briggs.

PETER M. SENGE

(b. 1947)

Systems thinking and the learning organization

Senior lecturer and director of the Center for Organizational Learning at Massachusetts Institute of Technology and the world's leading authority on organizational learning. His 1990 book *The Fifth Discipline* popularized the concept of the 'learning organization' in which individuals at all levels, including management, are enabled to develop their own skills, knowledge and competencies to the greater effectiveness of the whole. In one of Senge's definitions, a learning organization is 'continually expanding its capacity to create its future.'

The term had been coined a little earlier by the British consultant Bob Garratt in *The Learning Organization and the Need for Directors Who Think* (1987). Garratt followed it up in 1990 with a book called *Creating a Learning Organization*, but it was the MIT academic's work the same year, with the powerful resources of a leading US business school behind him, that focused widespread attention on the concept.

Senge's chief contribution was to identify five 'component technologies' or personal development techniques that go to make up a true learning organization. These were: personal mastery, mental models, shared vision, team learning and systems thinking – the latter, the 'fifth discipline,' being the ability to see the whole instead of the parts of an organization and to understand how individual actions can affect it. In 1997 *Harvard Business Review* described *The Fifth Discipline* as one of the seminal management books of the past 75 years.

Senge maintains a low personal profile, unusual among leading gurus, and disseminates little information about himself. He is chairman of the Society of Organizational Learning, a global virtual community of corporations, researchers and consultants dedicated to 'the interdependent development of people and their institutions.' He lectures internationally, holds somewhat 'new age'-style retreats for management (he is said to be a follower of Zen Buddhism) and works as a consultant in education, healthcare and government as well as business organizations. His research centre at MIT is partly sponsored by some of America's leading corporations, including Ford, AT&T and Motorola.

Originally an engineering graduate from Stanford, Senge has been at MIT since 1970 and freely acknowledges his debt to other pioneers in cognitive theory applied to organizations. Among them was Jay Forrester, a computer expert at MIT who got Senge interested in his theory of 'system dynamics' which propel organizations into certain paths of action.

Other powerful influences were Harvard professor Chris Argyris (qv), who originated the concept of single-loop and double-loop learning in his 1978 book, *Organizational Learning*, co-authored with MIT's Donald Schon, and the influential Arie de Geus, former head of planning at Shell, whom Senge credits with being the real progenitor of the learning organization. De Geus is also a seminal figure in the development of scenario planning and knowledge management and the author of one of the most-quoted aphorisms in management writing today: 'The ability to learn faster than your competitor may be the only sustainable competitive advantage.'

Senge was the first to preach that the most successful organizations of the future will be those that encourage learning at all levels and treat the skills, knowledge and experience of their employees as valuable assets – now a generally accepted truism. Managers, including the most senior executives, should regard themselves as stewards, teachers and designers of learning systems rather than top-down leaders. In a sequel to *The Fifth Discipline, entitled The Fifth Discipline Fieldbook* (1994), he presents practical tools for applying the principles in companies wanting to create their own learning organization.

Since 1990, the learning organization has become a key building block of change management. The theory has evolved and developed into such revolutionary but now familiar concepts as corporate 'universities', in-house personal development workshops and knowledge transfer driven by corporate intranets and other information systems.

Peter Senge enjoys a high reputation in a business world that has now adopted many of his teachings even if it remains sceptical as to what a learning organization is and whether it can be created. Increasingly, corporate learning and knowledge are seen as the key to survival, not merely competitiveness. Yet Senge's masterwork requires concentrated application: the reader must plough through a mass of conceptualizing in *The Fifth Discipline* to dig out the nuggets at the core, and there are more accessible and practical later books on the subject such as *The Power of Learning* by Andrew Mayo and Elizabeth Lank (1994), both then working at the British computer group ICL.

Senge's four 'disciplines' which are held together and informed by the fifth, 'systems thinking,' are broadly defined as follows:

- Personal mastery – the principle of continuous, lifelong learning by the individual, 'expanding the ability to produce the results we truly want in life'
- Mental models – uncovering and challenging those assumptions and mindsets that govern the individual's attitudes to the world
- Building shared vision – creating 'pictures of the future'

that bring people together in pursuit of a common goal
• Team learning – thinking and learning together as a group for more effective performance; this also enables members of the team to develop better than they would individually

Systems thinking is 'a framework for seeing interrelationships rather than linear cause-effect chains, and for seeing processes of change rather than static snapshots.' As an example of a problem in the late 1980s requiring systems thinking, Senge cited the US/USSR arms race, each segment of which connected into a vicious circle fuelling fear and aggression. Systems thinking, by seeing the cycle as a whole, would suggest that it could be run in reverse, by a unilateral move towards arms reductions – and that, Senge asserted, was just beginning to look possible in 1990 with the initiatives of USSR secretary-general Mikhail Gorbachev.

'The practice of systems thinking starts with understanding a simple concept called "feedback" that shows how actions can reinforce or counteract (balance) each other,' Senge writes in *The Fifth Discipline*. 'It builds to learning to recognize types of structures that recur again and again . . . Ultimately, it simplifies life by helping us see the deeper patterns lying behind the events and the details.'

All the disciplines are interrelated: 'If people do not share a common vision, and do not share common "mental models" about the business reality within which they operate, empowering people will only increase organizational stress and the burden of management to maintain coherence and direction.'

Senge's thinking on the mindsets that people hold about their work and organizations was deeply influenced by Chris Argyris' seminal discoveries about the 'defensive routines' that insulate individuals' habits of thought and protect them from upsetting confrontations. Watching Argyris one day conducting an informal workshop at MIT, Senge was struck by the thought that 'with proper training, I could become much more aware of my mental models and how they operated.' The experiences of businessmen with whom

200

he worked at MIT also led Senge to value the importance of openness among work colleagues and to understand the mental models through which people interpret the world – always incompletely.

Argyris' work with Donald Schon on double-loop learning and feedback – learning from others instead of relying on self-perpetuating experience – can also be seen as a key underlying component in Senge's development of systems thinking.

From outlining the development of individual cognitive skills, Senge moved on to redefine the role of management in a learning organization. One element was stewardship – guiding the ideas, core values and mission of the organization. But he also envisioned 'the manager as researcher and designer – researching the organization as a system and the forces, both internal and external, driving change, and designing the learning processes by which other managers throughout the organization come to understand the trends and forces as well.' This would be a key function of leadership in a learning organization, involving mentoring and coaching – a concept now widely accepted in management but radical in 1990.

If guiding the learning processes is not seen as the responsibility of corporate management, Senge warned, 'it will not be done, or it will not be done well. The fact that few of those presently in such positions recognize this role is one of the main reasons that learning organizations are still rare.'

Nearly a decade on, they are still rare, but pieces of them are beginning to fall into place.

KEY WRITINGS

Senge, P. (1990) *The Fifth Discipline: The Art and Practice of the Learning Organization*, New York: Doubleday; (1992) London: Century
Senge, P. (1994) T*he Fifth Discipline Fieldbook: Strategies for Building a Learning Organization*, New York: Doubleday; London: Nicholas Brealey.

ALFRED P. SLOAN

(1875–1966)

Decentralizing big corporations

US industrialist, head of General Motors from the early 1920s to the mid-1950s, and the man who virtually invented the decentralized, multi-divisional corporation of today. Sloan's name crops up more often in the indexes of management books than that of any other individual in industry – Peter Drucker's magisterial *Management: Tasks, Responsibilities, Practices* has over 25 page references to him.

Sloan wrote only one book, and that with assistance from a professional editor on *Fortune*; not usually enough to justify guru status in the management world, but that book, *My Years With General Motors* (1963), has been immensely influential on practising managers and on the study of organizations. James O'Toole, professor of management at the University of Southern California, called it 'the model for how managers should think – indeed, the model for much management education.' Sir John Egan, when he was chairman of Jaguar Cars, wrote in the preface to a new edition: 'I believe that this book should be on the reading list of everyone who can influence, or is influenced by, industrial enterprise.'

What was remarkable about Sloan's achievement in reorganizing the moribund General Motors of 1921 into America's leading automobile company within three years was not only that his innovations succeeded so quickly but that they have stood the test of decades of change and are still models of organizational thinking in a business world unrecognizable from that of 1921.

Twenty-five years after Sloan restructured GM, Henry Ford's grandson applied the same principles at Ford and within five years had regained the company's growth and profit potential. Nearly 30 years after Sloan's revolution, in the early 1950s, General Electric adapted his design and it became, in Peter Drucker's words, 'the standard model worldwide.'

An electrical engineer by training and a graduate of MIT (he later helped finance its Sloan School of Management), Sloan was the general manager of the Hyatt Roller Bearing Company in 1900, when it merged with United Motors. In 1917, United was acquired by General Motors and Sloan, by then United's president, joined the GM board. He became president in 1923, chairman in 1946 and honorary chairman from 1956 until his death ten years later.

Sloan's celebrated design for 'federal decentralization' – autonomous divisions subject to financial and policy controls from a small corporate staff – took him only one month to construct, working with a small committee of top GM executives. Pierre S. Du Pont, head of the chemical company which was a major shareholder in GM, had asked him to help pull GM back from the brink of bankruptcy, and Du Pont himself had earlier restructured his company along decentralized lines between 1915 and 1920; a fact which has led some management writers to assume that Sloan simply borrowed the idea.

In fact, the two firms had been suffering from opposing problems – Du Pont being heavily over-centralized, while GM was already untidily decentralized without adequate central control. In working out his own solution, Sloan greatly refined and polished the decentralization principle and, most importantly, developed the first systematic approaches to strategic planning. GM became the first company to change completely, through a planned strategy, the accepted manufacturing and marketing methods of an industry.

Such was the impact of this new approach that within ten years of the outbreak of World War I, the number of US automobile companies fell from over 100 to around a dozen, of which three (Ford, GM and Chrysler) accounted for fully 90 per cent of sales.

Alfred Pritchard Sloan, the Brooklyn-accented son of a New York tea, coffee and cigar wholesaler, was put in charge of General Motors in the midst of the worst slump to hit the infant automobile industry. William S. Durant had put together GM out of eight independent companies, all still run as virtual baronies by their owners, and it was plagued by over-production and wasteful duplication. Ford had 60 per cent of the US market with a single model – the Model T, cheap, standardized and black. General Motors had 12 per cent of the market with eight models, only two of which made a profit.

Sloan's 'federal' plan was designed to do more than rationalize GM's messy structure with centralized financial and policy control and professionally managed divisions each responsible for its own performance. It was to be the mechanism by which he could define and implement a new mission for GM – to produce a car for 'every purse and purpose.'

Up to that time the US auto industry was producing to just two levels of customer demand, the mass market and the class market; i.e. high-volume, low-priced cars, dominated by the Model T, and low-volume, high-priced cars. Sloan perceived much more varied and aspirational possibilities. He devised a five-model range, each overlapping in price and performance with the next, so that the low-income customer could pay a little more than for the Model T and get a car with far better styling and performance (and in other colours than black). At the same time, better-off purchasers could choose to economize with a good-looking low-priced car or pay slightly more and get a near-luxury model. Each of the five cars was designed to be a market leader in its class and competed with the GM car on either side of it, whether Chevrolet, Oldsmobile, Pontiac, Buick or Cadillac.

Sloan also introduced optional extras to stimulate customer interest, and by bringing in a new model every year he virtually invented the used-car market. This killed the changeless, all-alike Model T more quickly than any direct competition could have done. The one-year-old GM car, more stylish and a better performer than the Ford, could now beat it even on price.

The new organization Sloan devised reduced GM's eight car companies into five operating divisions, buttressed by three component divisions. Each division had its own engineering, production and sales departments but was supervised by a central corporate staff responsible for policy and finance. In every other way, each division was truly a business, with its chief executive responsible to Sloan as vice-president. (Sloan also introduced the innovation of taking a lower salary than the high-flyers who reported to him, the career professional). GM's accessory divisions sold both to the car divisions and to outside customers, including GM's competitors. This was a principle which has retained its value to the present day.

Sloan's ideas, in fact, were very largely based on the functional analysis of management drawn up by Henri Fayol in the previous century. Where Fayol had achieved the organizational solution for the single-product manufacturing business, Sloan accomplished it for the large, complex manufacturing business of the mass-production age.

Sloan introduced a system of checks and balances into the divisional structure that gave engineering, manufacturing and finance equal status. In time, however, his network of committees and policy groups, designed to produce impartial and even-handed decisions, became riddled with factions and the financial arm prevailed. Over-production ensued and GM's market share in the 1980s dropped by 15 per cent. Sloan's design has now had a rebuild, but it had served GM well for nearly 60 years.

Sloan was a firm believer in the impersonal, task-focused concept of management. He was also an early believer in encouraging the sort of creative dissent that Tom Peters (qv) and Richard Pascale (qv) are recommending for keeping companies vigorous and innovative in the 1990s. Peter Drucker and other management writers like to quote a story about Sloan chairing a meeting of one of GM's top committees. At the end of the discussion, he said: 'Gentlemen, I take it we are all in complete agreement on the decision here.' Everyone round the table nodded. 'Then,' said Sloan, 'I propose we postpone further discussion of this matter until the next meeting to give ourselves time to develop disagreement, and perhaps gain some understanding of what the decision is all about.'

Sloan was almost alone among practising managers before World War II to evolve management theories that have become classics. The other well-known example is Chester Barnard of American Telephone. But Sloan's achievements, though renowned throughout the automobile industry, only became widely known in 1963 when he published *My Years With General Motors*. The book became one of the first best-selling management autobiographies.

By this time, however, Sloan was nearly 90 and the book, it must be said, is no racy read along the lines of an Iacocca or Geneen. It is formal, old-fashioned and sometimes pedantic in style; nevertheless it provides a matchlessly detailed and authentic picture of how US industry was run between the wars. No one else could have produced so authoritative a case study as this man who, born in 1875, had grown up with the automobile and very largely shaped its place in modern American life.

The essentials of Sloan's organizational genius, however, can be more clearly picked out in books by others – Drucker's *Managing for Results*, for example, or his *Concept of the Corporation*. *My Years With General Motors* is best read as a slice of nutritious if sometimes dry industrial and social history.

KEY WRITING

Sloan, A. P. (1963, 1966, 1986) *My Years With General Motors*, New York: Doubleday; London: Sidgwick and Jackson; Penguin Books.

F. W. TAYLOR

(1856–1915)

Scientific management and 'the one best way'

The man with a strong claim to being America's first management consultant, Frederick Winslow Taylor was the Quaker engineer who invented scientific management, the forerunner of time and motion study, work study and to some extent, business process re-engineering. Unlike most of the consultants who followed him, Taylor was at home on the factory floor, and invented a machine tool that revolutionized the steel industry.

He spent his industrial career in steel companies, starting as a humble labourer with the Midvale Steel Works, where he ended as chief engineer, and then moving to the Bethlehem Steel Works of Pittsburgh as a consulting engineer in management. It was here that he carried out his celebrated experiments in breaking down the components of a manual task, timing each movement with a stopwatch. By finding the 'one best way' to perform every action in loading a railway car with pig-iron, he enabled a labourer called Henry Noll to lift his productivity from 12.5 tons to 47 tons a day. When applied to bricklaying, the technique was found to increase performance from 1,000 to 2,700 bricks a day.

Taylor believed that every employee could be trained to be 'first-class' at some job, and that it was management's responsibility to identify these possibilities and provide opportunities for improvement.

Even at college, where he was nicknamed 'Speedy,' Taylor was obsessed with improving efficiency. He got the rules of baseball changed by proving that over-arm bowling was more effective than under-arm. He was less successful, however, in persuading the tennis authorities that a spoon-shaped racket was more efficient than an oval one.

His revolutionary book, *Principles of Scientific Management*, was developed out of academic papers published in the *American Magazine* in the spring of 1911. The book that followed was subsequently reissued as *Scientific Management* in 1947. A British army officer, Major Lyndall Urwick, reading Taylor in the trenches of the First World War, was inspired to found a movement for scientific management in Britain: he later became the UK's first professional management consultant.

Scientific management had a great vogue in Fascist Italy, the Soviet Union and Nazi Germany, where its methodology may even have influenced the death camps. According to a recent biography of Taylor, one German historian has described Adolf Eichmann as 'a perfect Taylor engineer.'

In the US, Taylor's work was carried forward and developed as time and motion study by the husband-and-wife team Frank and Lillian Gilbreth and other industrial psychologists. Japanese industrialists have admired Taylor since 1913 and adopted many of his principles in developing revolutionary production techniques in the 1970s and 1980s: Taiichi Ohno of Toyota, father of the just-in-time system, acknowledged his debt to scientific management.

Taylor's influence can be strongly detected in business process re-engineering, that dominant management fad of the mid-1990s, and it is interesting to note that, much as re-engineering was initially criticized for de-humanising work processes, so Taylor in his own day was attacked for stripping jobs of skill and judgement, and for treating workers as machine parts. 'After (Henry) Ford and Taylor got through with them,' notes Taylor's biographer Robert Kanigel, 'most jobs needed less of everything – less brains, less muscle, less independence.'

From management's point of view, Taylorism in its heyday stood for efficiency and the elimination of waste. It powered US production techniques in World War II and its principles can be seen today in any industry based on standardized production and quality, such as the fast-food business.

In 1977 three groups of US historians and managers ranked Taylor first among contributors to American business and management thought – Ford came no higher than sixth. In 1994 the revered Peter Drucker (qv) reasserted his view that Taylor, Darwin and Freud were the makers of the modern world.

For all its flaws, Taylorism remains a powerful, if unacknowledged force in the insatiable management search, sharpened by the recession of the early 1990s, for doing more with less.

Frederick W. Taylor believed in one maxim above all, that 'the principal object of management should be to secure the maximum prosperity for the employer, coupled with the maximum prosperity of each employee.' To this end he preached that management and workforce were interdependent and relied on each other to achieve the common goal of higher prosperity. An early experiment as consultant to a ball-bearing company on raising the quality of their product was conducted on the principle of a modern quality with the workers becoming responsible for their own improvement.

Other ideas of his, such as performance measurement – albeit in primitive form in the 1900s – have stood the test of time, but his arrogance in controlling how people worked caused a lasting counter-revolution half a century later, when it became understood that performance was directly linked to motivation, participation and satisfying a worker's sense of self-worth. Taylor deeply antagonized the labour unions by making peak productivity gains (such as Noll's 47 tons) the norm, with penalties for falling short.

His writing exhibited a certain blinkered complacency. 'Under scientific management,' Taylor wrote, 'the initiative of the workmen – that is, their hard work, their good will, their ingenuity – is obtained practically with absolute regularity, while under even the best of the older type of management the initiative is only obtained spasmodically and somewhat irregularly . . . By far the greater gain under scientific management comes from the new, the very great and the extraordinary burdens and duties which are voluntarily assumed by those on the management's side.'*

Principles of Scientific Management rested on four 'great underlying principles of management.' These were:

1. The development of a science of work to replace the old rule-of-thumb methods by which workmen operated. Fulfilling optimum goals would earn higher wages; failure to do so would result in loss of earnings.
2. Scientific selection and progressive development of the worker: training each to be 'first-class' at some task.
3. Bringing together the science of work and the scientifically selected and trained workers for best results.
4. Equal division of work and responsibility between workers and management, cooperating together in close interdependence.

In Taylor's thinking, every task, whether of worker or manager, became discrete and specialized. In its application to management, he described this as 'functional management.' On the worker's side, he saw benefits of increased earnings, by between 30 and 100 per cent.

Taylor and Ford between them set the mould for mass production and the assembly line – although Ford always denied the influence of scientific management on his factories, other car manufacturers were adopting Taylor's methods years before Ford's first assembly line cranked into action in 1913, and reporting substantial cuts in costs and

*F. W. Taylor (1947) *Scientific Management*, New York: Harper and Row, quoted in *Organization Theory*, (1990) ed. D. S. Pugh, London: Penguin Books.

manpower.

'In the past the man was first,' wrote Taylor in *Principles of Scientific Management*. 'In the future the system will be first.' Although his theories are now ostensibly discredited, they have resilient powers of survival. Robert Waterman, the co-author of *In Search of Excellence* and author of two respected books examining how companies renew themselves and enhance their performance through people management, believes that many managers in the late 1990s are Taylorists at heart.

And, as Peter Drucker acknowledged in his monumental book *Management: Tasks, Responsibilities, Practices* (1974), Taylor was 'the first man in history who did not take work for granted, but looked at it and studied it.'

KEY WRITINGS

Taylor, F. W. (1947) *Scientific Management*, New York: Harper and Row.

Recommended background reading: *The One Best Way: Frederick Winslow Taylor and the Enigma of Efficiency*, by Robert Kanigel (Viking, New York and John Wiley, London, 1997).

MAX WEBER

(1864–1920)

How individuals respond to authority in organizations

German sociologist and political economist, trained as a lawyer, who taught at Berlin University and later became professor of economics at the universities of Freiburg, Heidelberg and Munich. In 1918 he was a member of the committee set up to draft the constitution of the Weimar Republic. His widest-read book was – and remains – *The Protestant Ethic and The Spirit of Capitalism*, a short and stimulating thesis that linked the moral imperatives of puritanical Protestantism, especially Calvinism, with the mainspring of entrepreneurial capitalism, the pursuit of profit and, ultimately, with the 'iron cage' of modern materialism. Weber's chief interest to students of management and organization theory – though now much less influential than it used to be – lies in *The Theory of Social and Economic Organisation*, first published in 1924, four years after his death.

Max Weber was the first writer on management theory to analyse the role of the leader in an organization and to examine how and why individuals respond to various forms of authority. He was probably the first, since the Greeks coined the term, to use 'charisma' in its modern sense of that quality in an individual's personality which effortlessly draws others to follow.

Weber distinguished three types of legitimate authority, as opposed to power, which forces people to obey: the rational, the traditional and the charismatic. The rational, or rational-legal, which he saw as the dominant form of modern institution, rested on a system of rationally thought-out goals and functions designed to maximize the performance of an organization and implemented by certain rules and procedures. Authority here was vested in the office of a person rather than in the individual. It was an impersonal system which he described, with no criticism implied, as a bureaucracy. He held a bureaucracy to be the most efficient form of administration because it worked on a commonly accepted hierarchical basis without personal whim and with a judicious reliance on the appointment of experts.

The traditional form of authority in organizations was seen by Weber as being owed to the person rather than the office; typically, a hereditary system where the leader's writ is established by precedent, as in a family business. It has roots in feudal rights and duties but is not unknown in modern firms where patronage may take the place of inheritance. Weber's concept of tradition may also be detected in the cultures of those companies where the attitude 'we've always done it this way' becomes a self-justification resistant to critical analysis by newcomers.

Charismatic authority, because it relies on the particular qualities of an individual, is unlikely to find a successor in its own mould. Organizations with charismatic founders like Henry Ford or Thomas J. Watson of IBM tend to mutate, either into the traditional (hereditary) mode, with greater or lesser success, or into a succession determined by impersonal factors and hence into a rational, bureaucratic form.

Weber was in no doubt that the latter system was the buttress of efficient administration in whatever kind of institution it operates. 'Precision, speed, unambiguity, knowledge of files, continuity, discretion, unity, strict subordination, reduction of friction and of material and personal costs – these are raised to the optimum point in the strictly bureaucratic administration,' he wrote.

214

The system's machine-like superiority over other types of authority rests on its hierarchical form, with each office subordinate to the one above it; every official's role determined by written rules; a regulated right of appeal and the ability to take grievances upwards; and complete separation of the administrative staff from ownership of the means of production or administration, as well as a complete absence of 'rights' to any office by its incumbent.

The purest type of bureaucratic administration, says Weber, exists when its officials conduct the business according to ten criteria:

1. They are personally free, subject only to authority in respect of their impersonal official obligations.
2. They are organized in a clearly defined hierarchy of offices.
3. Each office has a clearly defined sphere of competence in the legal sense.
4. The office is filled by a free, contractual relationship. Thus, in principle, there is free selection.
5. Candidates are selected on the basis of technical qualifications. In the most rational case, this is tested by examination or guaranteed by diplomas certifying technical training, or both. They are appointed, not elected.
6. They are remunerated by fixed salaries in money, for the most part with a right to pensions. Only under certain circumstances does the employing authority, especially in private organizations, have a right to terminate the appointment, but the official is always free to resign. The salary scale is primarily graded according to rank in the hierarchy; but in addition to this criterion, the responsibility of the position and the requirements of the incumbent's social status may be taken into account.
7. The office is treated as the sole, or at least the primary, occupation of the incumbent.
8. It constitutes a career. There is a system of 'promotion' according to seniority or to achievement, or to both. Promotion is dependent on the judgment of superiors.
9. The official works entirely separated from ownership of the means of administration, and without appropriation

of his position.
10. He is subject to strict and systematic discipline and control in the conduct of the office.*

Weber's ten criteria are in the process of being dismantled
in much contemporary management thinking, such as the
work of Charles Handy and Rosabeth Moss Kanter, who
anticipate a sea-change in both the hierarchical nature of
organizations and the concept of life-long bureaucratic
careers. But a century ago, Weber was utterly convinced of
the superiority of this form of harnessing the corporate
effort of individuals, and many an organization in the 1990s
testifies to its durability:

'Experience tends universally to show that the purely
bureaucratic type of administrative organization – that is,
the monocratic variety of bureaucracy – is, from a purely
technical point of view, capable of attaining the highest
degree of efficiency and is in this sense formally the most
rational known means of carrying out imperative control
over human beings. It is superior to any other form in precision, in stability, in the stringency of its discipline, and in
its reliability. It thus makes possible a particularly high
degree of calculability of results for the heads of the organization and for those acting in relation to it. It is finally
superior both in intensive efficiency and in the scope of its
operations, and is formally capable of application to all kinds
of administrative tasks.'*

*Taken from *The Theory of Social and Economic Organisation*, translated
and edited by A. M. Henderson and T. Parsons, New York: Free Press.
Quoted in *Organization Theory* (1990) edited by D. S. Pugh, London:
Penguin Books.

KEY WRITINGS

Weber, M. (1930) *The Protestant Ethic and the Spirit of Capitalism*, London: Allen and Unwin.
Weber, M. (1947) *The Theory of Social and Economic Organisation*, New York: The Free Press.

GLOSSARY OF
MANAGEMENT TERMS

Action learning
A system of management education, invented by the British
guru Reg Revans, in which a group of working managers
learn by discussing each other's practical problems.

Adhocracy
The opposite of bureaucracy: a term originally coined by
Warren Bennis and subsequently adopted by Alvin Toffler,
Henry Mintzberg and Robert Waterman to describe small,
flexible project teams or groups that operate freely across
the departmental boundaries of an organization.

Balanced Scorecard
System of measuring an organization's performance, balancing financial and important non-financial areas such as customer satisfaction, cycle-time improvements and learning
capabilities. The quadrant design of the scorecard, invented
by Harvard professor Robert S. Kaplan and consultant
David Norton, enables any business to tailor it to its own
needs.

Career anchor
Term coined by Edgar Schein to denote the perceptions
that individuals hold about themselves in their jobs – and
which encourage them to stay in those jobs.

Champions
Influential individuals, often in research-based companies, whose backing can ensure that a project or invention gets the chance to prove itself. Peters and Waterman's *In Search of Excellence* found that companies which nurtured champions were more likely to qualify as excellent.

Competitive advantage
The factor that enables a company to gain an edge on its rivals in the marketplace, the result of **competitive strategy**. Harvard's Michael Porter has worked out a sophisticated formula for determining how companies – and countries – can gain competitive advantage.

Core competencies
What a company does well – the portfolio of skills, technologies and capabilities that give it power to attract customers and a competitive advantage over its market rivals. The term is associated with Gary Hamel and C. K. Prahalad, whose 1994 book *Competing for the Future* stressed the need for managers to think about building core competencies for markets years ahead.

Decentralization
The principle (first recognized in management writing by Alfred D. Chandler but put into practice decades before, in the early 1920s, by Alfred P. Sloan at General Motors) of devolving substantial amounts of managerial power and accountability away from the centre of a large and diverse corporation to semi-autonomous divisions or business units. After Sloan's book was published in 1963, decentralization became the vogue among large industrial conglomerates.

Empowerment
The fashionable managerial buzzword of the early 1990s. In organizations it is usually taken to mean increased participation by employees in the enterprise for which they work, with a view to stimulating initiative and entrepreneurism. It has particular implications for women in eroding the invisible barriers that tend to keep them in mundane

organizational roles. Rosabeth Moss Kanter is the leading exponent of empowerment as an aid to releasing forces for innovation and change within a corporation.

Hierarchy of needs
Motivation model constructed by Abraham Maslow which charts the progression of human needs in the workplace from basic urges of warmth, food and safety to love, esteem and personal fulfilment. Maslow teaches that none of the wants is absolute: that, indeed, a satisfied want ceases to be important.

Job enrichment
Enhancing work by motivational factors that meet employees' aspirations in (usually) non-monetary ways. Frederick Herzberg, who coined the concept, said wryly that it had 'given employment to a hell of a lot of consultants'.

Just-in-time
Revolutionary Japanese low-inventory system for speeding up production, keeping it flexible to customers' requirements and cutting costs. Suppliers supply what is needed *when* it is needed, resulting in faster responses to the market.

Knowledge management
The art of capturing and deploying – through well managed information technology – the accumulated expertise and experience of the individuals working in an organization to enable it to be shared and maximized for better performance. First promoted by the Swedish financial services group Skandia, the idea became big in the US in the late 1990s with corporations appointing 'chief knowledge officers' or 'chief information officers' – sometimes simply renaming the IT director. Associated with this is 'intellectual capital', an acknowledgment that a company's prime assets reside in the brains of its employees.

Lateral thinking
Defined by the *Oxford English Dictionary* as 'seeking to solve problems by unorthodox or apparently illogical methods'.

Inventor Edward de Bono, who has applied the principle to dozens of challenging situations, including management, describes its purpose as 'the generation of new ideas and the escape from old ones'.

Learning organization
Linked to knowledge management, the learning organization is a coinage variously attributed to former Shell planning director Arie de Geus, British consultant Bob Garratt and MIT's Peter Senge, who made the concept fashionable. The idea is for an organization to enable individual employees to develop their full capabilities and creativity in order to enhance the performance of the whole. Learning is both internal and external – about the company, its competitors, its customers and the environment in which it operates. Whether an entire learning organization exists anywhere is debatable, but successful spin-offs include corporate 'universities' and mechanisms for tapping employees' problem-solving potential such as General Electric's 'Work-Out' sessions.

Management by objectives
In its heyday in the 1970s, MBO divides corporate goals into objectives that can be assigned to individual managers and measured against performance. Like many other seminal ideas, MBO originated in the fertile mind of Peter Drucker, but was enlarged and developed into a practical methodology in the late 1960s and early 1970s by the British management consultant John Humble.

Managerial hierarchies
The analysis of bureaucratic administration, with each office subordinate to the one above it and every official's role determined by his office, was first undertaken by Max Weber. Alfred Chandler carried it further in his studies of the executive function in great US corporations, arguing that the way an organization's hierarchy operates is determined by its strategic goals. Many of today's gurus, led by Rosabeth Moss Kanter, Charles Handy and the indestructible Peter Drucker, predict that the future will see flatter,

non-hierarchical management structures in which the 'boss' principle is less important than empowering a wide range of contributory talents.

Mission statement
The distillation of a company's philosophy and corporate goals and values. It can range in length from a sentence to a book (viz. the IBM classic, *A Business and Its Beliefs*, by Thomas J. Watson, Jr., son of the firm's founder).

Motivational theories
Management theory underwent a sea-change in the 1930s when scientific management, emphasizing measurement of task and performance, gave way to social psychology and human relations, emphasizing the role and motivation of the individual. Elton Mayo, in his seminal work at Western Electric's Hawthorne plant in Chicago in the late 1920s and early 1930s, was the first to identify psychological elements leading to increased productivity. Later theories have included the hierarchy of needs (qv) and the psychological contract (qv), but all have stressed the importance of the peer group in job satisfaction and self-esteem.

Portfolio work
Charles Handy's attractive view of the future for many 'knowledge workers', who, as long-term careers in one organization become rarer, will increasingly divide their time into two, three or more discretionary areas of work. Some may be voluntary (e.g. part-time clergy) or otherwise unpaid (e.g. mature student), but have the potential to enhance the quality of the individual's life and personal development.

Psychological contract
Term coined by Edgar Schein to denote what an employee may expect from his or her employer – less in material rewards than in the opportunities to realize potential. It applies also to the employer's expectations of those who work for an organization.

Quality management
How production faults can be eliminated by a management-led philosophy of continuous improvement in every process of planning, production and service. W. Edwards Deming laid down the principle that all processes are vulnerable to loss of quality through variations but that the levels of variation can be managed in order to raise quality consistency. Both Deming and fellow quality guru Joseph Juran insist that quality control starts at the top: Deming believed that 85 per cent of production faults are the responsibility of management.

Re-engineering or Business Process Redesign (BPR)
Described by Michael Hammer, the MIT computer scientist who made it the big idea of the early 1990s, as 'reversing the industrial revolution,' re-engineering was a mix of techniques from just-in-time back to F. W. Taylor's time and motion study, designed to streamline work processes across departments, take out costs and raise productivity. In practice, it was used by many firms to 'downsize' and ended up cutting muscle as well as fat, leaving companies unable to grow as markets came out of recession. Reaction against its mechanistic nature caused the advocates of re-engineering to look more closely at the human dimension. People rather than processes are now seen as the key to successful change.

Seven 'S' model
The system devised by the then McKinsey team of Richard Pascale, Tom Peters and Robert Waterman to measure the quality of a company's performance: the seven 'S' factors divide into three 'hard' – strategy, structure and systems – and four 'soft' – style, shared values, skills and staff. Pascale used the model in *The Art of Japanese Management* in case studies comparing US and Japanese companies; Peters and Waterman employed it for *In Search of Excellence*.

Theory X and Theory Y
The terms coined by Douglas McGregor to epitomize two diametrically opposed sets of management assumptions whose roots go back to Plato and Aristotle. Theory X

assumes that most human beings are lazy, dislike work and responsibility and need to be firmly directed; Theory Y that they actively want to work, achieve and assume responsibility, and should be allowed more self-direction. Before his death in 1964 McGregor was evolving a refined 'Theory Z', but this term was later adopted and adapted by William Ouchi in his book of that title.

Vertical integration
The system favoured by some large corporations for integrating a number of companies down to supplier level to act as an in-house chain of manufacture. Once an established and successful strategy of the US automobile industry, its weaknesses are now more clearly seen as companies have learned that they can't be equally good at a variety of activities. 'Partnering' suppliers rather than integrating them is now the vogue.

RECOMMENDED GENERAL READING

Pugh, D. S. and Hickson, D. J. eds (1990, 4th edition): *Writers on Organizations*, London: Penguin.

Key readings from the works of gurus who have contributed to the study of organizations, including 17 of the thinkers in *Guide to the Management Gurus*.

Pugh, D. S. ed (1990, 3rd edition) *Organization Theory: Selected Readings*, London: Penguin.

Helpfully chosen tastings from important writings including McGregor's Theory X and Y, Mayo on the Hawthorne experiments and key articles by Mintzberg and R.M. Kanter.

Clutterbuck, David and Crainer, Stuart (1990) *Makers of Management*, London: Macmillan.

Stimulating history of management ideas and the people who evolved them, both academics and industrialists, with a useful chronology of management thinking and an excellent bibliography.

Micklethwait, J. and Wooldridge, A. (1996) *The Witch*

Doctors, London: Heinemann.

Stylish, incisive and entertaining dissection of the management advice industry, including gurus 'on the wild side' such as Stephen Covey, by two leading *Economist* writers.

Kennedy, Carol (1994) *Managing with the Gurus*, London: Century

The companion to this book: a selection of the best writing on 20 key managerial functions, with linking commentaries on the development of ideas in each field.

ACKNOWLEDGEMENTS

Extracts from *The Mind of the Strategist*, by Kenichi Ohmae (McGraw-Hill, 1982) and *The Human Side of Enterprise*, by Douglas McGregor (McGraw-Hill, 1960) reproduced by permission of McGraw-Hill, Inc.

Quotation from *Corporate Strategy*, by H. Igor Ansoff, (McGraw-Hill, New York, 1965, Sidgwick and Jackson, London, 1986) reproduced by permission of Dr. H. I. Ansoff.

Excerpt from *In Search of Excellence*, by Thomas J. Peters and Robert H. Waterman Jr. (Harper and Row, 1982) reproduced by permission of HarperCollins Publishers.

Excerpts from *The Art of Japanese Management*, by Richard Pascale and Anthony Athos (Simon and Schuster, 1981) and *Managing on the Edge*, by Richard Pascale (Simon and Schuster, 1990) reproduced by permission of Simon and Schuster, Inc.

W. E. Deming's 'Fourteen Points' extracted from *The Deming Dimension* by Henry Neave (SPC Press, 1990) and reproduced by permission of SPC Press Inc., Knoxville, Tennessee.